THE PRINCE OF PARTHIA

A Tragedy

Five hundred and eighty copies of *The Prince of Parthia*, of which five hundred and fifty are for sale, have been printed from type and the type distributed.

This copy is Number 64

Schooner Charming Nancy, J. Mullowny to Halifax.

By Authority.

NEVER PERFORMED BEFORE.

By the AMERICAN COMPANY,

At the NEW THEATRE, in *Southwark*,

On *FRIDAY*, the *Twenty-Fourth* of *April*, will be presented, A TRAGEDY written by the late ingenious Mr. *Thomas Godfrey*, of this city, called the

PRINCE *of* PARTHIA.

The PRINCIPAL CHARACTERS by Mr. HALLAM, Mr. DOUGLASS, Mr. WALL, Mr. MORRIS, Mr. ALLYN, Mr. TOMLINSON, Mr. BROADBELT, Mr. GREVILLE, Mrs. DOUGLASS, Mrs. MORRIS, Miss WAINWRIGHT, and Miss CHEER.

To which will be added, A *Ballad Opera* called

The CONTRIVANCES,

To begin exactly at *Seven* o'Clock.--*Vivant Rex & Regina.*

April 23.

TO BE LETT,

TWO pasture LOTTS, situated near the Lower Ferry road,

ANNOUNCEMENT OF FIRST PRODUCTION

From the *Pennsylvania Journal*, April 23, 1767

THE PRINCE OF PARTHIA

A TRAGEDY

BY

THOMAS GODFREY

EDITED WITH INTRODUCTION, HISTORICAL, BIOGRAPHICAL, AND CRITICAL

BY

ARCHIBALD HENDERSON

BOSTON
LITTLE, BROWN, AND COMPANY
1917

TO

JAMES SPRUNT

CHRONICLER OF THE CAPE FEAR

IN GRATEFUL ACKNOWLEDGEMENT OF

UNFLAGGING STIMULATION AND GENIAL AID

PREFATORY NOTE

In commemoration of the one hundred and fiftieth anniversary of the first and only professional production of "The Prince of Parthia" in 1767, this play is now published for the first time since its original publication in 1765. The text is reproduced without variation from the original.

For valuable assistance rendered me in connection with the present edition, I take pleasure in acknowledging, first of all, my exceptional indebtedness to Mr. James Sprunt of Wilmington, North Carolina. In greater or less degree, I am indebted for assistance to Mr. William B. McKoy of Wilmington; to Mr. Joseph Jackson and Mr. E. P. Oberholtzer of Philadelphia; to Professor A. H. Quinn of the University of Pennsylvania; and to Mr. and Mrs. Guernsey Moore of Swarthmore, Pennsylvania — to all of whom my hearty thanks are expressed.

ARCHIBALD HENDERSON

"Fordell", Chapel Hill, North Carolina,
December, 1916.

TABLE OF CONTENTS

LIST OF PLATES

THE PRINCE OF PARTHIA

A TRAGEDY

INTRODUCTION

THOMAS GODFREY

AND

"THE PRINCE OF PARTHIA"

WHETHER or not it be true, as is so frequently asserted, that America has produced little drama worthy of the name, certain it is that such drama as America has produced, especially in the early period of our history, languishes in obscurity for lack of popular interest and critical interpretation. A conspicuous instance of the neglect of our native drama is afforded in "The Prince of Parthia", published for the first and only time a century and a half ago. In cyclopedia and biographical dictionary, there is no dearth of feeble and inadequate accounts of Thomas Godfrey. Yet in the mind of no biographer has significance been accorded to the circumstance that this noteworthy beginning of American drama was made in Wilmington, North Carolina; that it was here the first American tragedy was brought to completion; that it was from this place that the manuscript of this work of original genius was despatched to Godfrey's native city, Philadelphia, for subsequent production — the first production of a native tragedy upon the professional stage in America;

and that it is here Godfrey sleeps unhonored and unsung in an unmarked grave. It is surely incumbent upon the student of our native drama, concerned with the larger interests of our national literature, to endeavor to discover the circumstances under which the play was written and, if possible, to re-create in imagination the literary and cultural conditions of American society, in Philadelphia and in Wilmington, in which young Godfrey found sympathy and encouragement for creative effort. Such a study is especially appropriate at a time when the entire civilized world is paying a monumental international tribute to the genius of William Shakespeare; for this, Godfrey's only dramatic work, is the rich fruit of Shakespearean study.

I.

There is reason for genuine regret that no detailed and authoritative study has ever been made, so far as is known, of the rare composite of scientist and artist — bipartite genius of the type of José Echegaray or "Lewis Carroll", for example — who combines in mediately even proportions the powers of scientific analysis and creative imagination. Little less interesting than this type is the case of the literary artist who is the offspring of the scientist — afforded us in the example of Thomas Godfrey, Jr., the poet, son of Thomas Godfrey, Sr., the mathematician.

Thomas Godfrey, Senior, was born in Bristol township, about one mile from Germantown, in the colony of Pennsylvania, in the year 1704, on a farm adjoining Lukens' mill, on the Church lane. In some notes on the Godfrey family, J. F. Watson says: "His grandfather, Thomas Godfrey, a farmer, had purchased the place of 153 acres from Samuel Carpenter, merchant of Philadelphia, on the 24th of August, 1697. His father, Joseph, a farmer and maltster, died in 1705, when he was but one year old. His mother afterwards married one Wood, of Philadelphia, and put her son out to learn the business of a glazier. The glaziers then did not paint as now; they only soldered the glasses into leaden frames. He did such work for the State house in 1732–3. He also did the same for £6 10*s*. for Andrew Hamilton's house at Bush hill, in 1740 — and I saw his bills. His father's estate became his when he was of age. He appears to have sold it to John Lukens on the 1st of January, 1735. The same premises sold in 1812 for $30,600." [1] According to traditionary accounts, Thomas Godfrey, the "American glazier", was both poor and uneducated; and the "authors" of the *American Magazine* [2] have given this flowery description of him, fully characteristic of the fanciful writing of the period: "Nature seems not to have designed the Father for a greater Mathematician, than she has the son for a Poet. The former, was, perhaps, one of the most singular Phænomena that ever appeared in the learned world. For without the least advantages of education, almost intuitively, and in a manner entirely his own, he had made himself master of the abstrusest parts of Mathematics and Astronomy." It is clear that he was a man of some small property and moderately well-to-do; and the business in which he was engaged, of glazier or plumber, was reasonably

[1] Watson: "Annals of Philadelphia", 1850 edition, I, 528.
[2] September, 1758.

profitable. His interest early turning toward mathematical science, through the mere chance of reading a mathematical work, he resolutely set to work to educate himself. As an illustration of his pertinacity in acquiring knowledge, it is related that, being baffled by the Latin terms with which mathematical books were interspersed, Godfrey "applied himself to that language with such diligence as to be able to read the occasional Latin he found." The branches of mathematics for which he showed the greatest fondness and aptitude were optics and astronomy.[1]

Intimate personal glimpses of the man and his family are given us by Benjamin Franklin, with all his forthright simplicity and engaging naïveté. After his return, at the age of twenty-one, from his sojourn in London, young Franklin took a house "near the Market" in Philadelphia; and with characteristic frugality, in order to lessen the rent, he and his partner, Hugh Meredith, a "Welsh Pensilvanian", thirty years of age, "took in Thomas Godfrey . . . and his family, who were to pay a considerable part of it to us, and we to board with them." [2] In the autumn of 1727 the studious Franklin formed most of his "ingenious acquaintances" into a "club for mutual improve-

[1] Watson, l. c., I, 529–530. *Cf.* also "Philosophical Transactions", No. 435, and Watson's Ms. "Annals", p. 566, in the Historical Society of Pennsylvania.

[2] "Works of Benjamin Franklin", edited by John Bigelow, Phila., 1887, I, 140. In 1730 Meredith removed to North Carolina with many other Welsh settlers from Pennsylvania, who were induced to go on account of the cheapness of the lands. Somewhat later, Franklin published in his newspaper, the *Pennsylvania Gazette,* two letters written by Meredith from North Carolina, containing, as Franklin said, "the best account that had been given of that country, the climate, soil, husbandry, etc." — l. c., 152.

ment", which he named the Junto. "The rules that I drew up", says Franklin in his "Autobiography", "required that every member in his turn should produce one or more queries on any point of Morals, Politics, or Natural Philosophy, to be discuss'd by the company; and once in three months produce and read an essay of his own writing, on any subject he pleased."[1] Among the first members was Thomas Godfrey, one of the directors of the Library Company of Philadelphia, whom Franklin described in the following thumb-nail sketch: ". . . a self-taught mathematician, great in his way, and afterwards inventor of what is now called Hadley's Quadrant, . . . he knew little out of his way, and was not a pleasing companion; as, like most great mathematicians I have met with, he expected universal precision in everything said, or was for ever denying or distinguishing upon trifles, to the disturbance of all conversation." The diplomatic Mrs. Godfrey endeavored to arrange a match between Franklin and one of her relations; but the negotiations finally resulted in the departure of the Godfreys in a huff. After a "serious courtship" of the young girl, who he acknowledges with comical condescension to have been "very deserving", Franklin let Mrs. Godfrey, the go-between, know that "he expected as much money with their daughter as would pay off his debt for the printing-house", which he computed as not above a hundred pounds. After that,

[1] "Works of Franklin." Edited by John Bigelow, 1887, I, 142. For an interesting description of the Junto, see the paper read before the American Philosophical Society by Dr. Patterson, one of its vice-presidents, on the 25th of May, 1843, in commemoration of its Centennial Anniversary.

Franklin pregnantly observes, "I resolved to take no more inmates."[1]

II.

Extended researches in Philadelphia and in the archives of the Royal Society of England abundantly demonstrate that Godfrey independently invented the instrument which Hadley afterwards improved. Of the invention, made in the year 1730, the following interesting anecdote is related: "Godfrey, who followed in our city the trade of a glazier, was one day engaged in replacing a pane of glass in the window of a house on the North side of Mulberry Street. A girl who had filled a pail with water, at a pump, that stood opposite, placed it on the sidewalk, and Godfrey, on turning towards it, saw the sun which had first been reflected from the window on which he was working, into the bucket of water, and a second time from the surface of the water to his eyes. His philosophical mind seized at once upon the observation and the principle was thus applied to the construction of an instrument with which he could draw the sun down to the horizon by means of a contrivance incomparably superior to any that had ever been used for the purpose of ascertaining angular measurements."[2] The incident

[1] "Works of Franklin," I, 165, 167. In the earliest article on Thomas Godfrey, Sr. which I have discovered in any North Carolina publication, an article copied from the Petersburg (Va.) *Intelligencer*, he is described as "a Glazier who carried his box of glass, putty, hammer, and knife on his arm, and went through the streets of Philadelphia, to mend or replace broken panes in windows." *Western Carolinian*, Salisbury, N. C., August 28, 1821.

[2] An Address delivered at Laurel Hill Cemetery on the completion of a monument erected to the memory of Thomas Godfrey, June 1st, 1843, by G. Emerson, M. D. In the communication above cited, in the Petersburg

THE YOUNG FRANKLIN
From the sculpture by R. Tait McKenzie

has additional significance, in that, by one of those odd chances upon which momentous events sometimes hinge, Godfrey thereby attracted the interest and won the friendship of the famous James Logan. Indeed, the incident described above took place while working on the premises at Logan's place, Stenton. The train of reflection thus excited — "by accidently observing a piece of fallen glass," says Watson, probably erroneously — "caused him to quit his scaffold and to go into Mr. Logan's library, where he took down a volume of Newton. Mr. Logan entering at this time and seeing the book in his hand, inquired into the motive of his search, when he was exceedingly pleased with Godfrey's ingenuity, and from that time became his zealous friend." The distinguished Logan, patron of literature and science, and the correspondent of such eminent scientists as Linnæus, Fabricius, Peter Collinson, and William Jones, in May, 1732 addressed a letter to Dr. Edmund Halley, President of the Royal Society of London, setting forth Godfrey's claims to recognition as the original inventor of the quadrant.[1] "Mr. Logan proves most conclusively," says Dr. Emerson, "that the Quadrant was not only invented in our city (Philadelphia), . . . but was actually in use (in 1730) two years prior to Hadley's claim."

Intelligencer, the writer, who signs himself "H", states that Godfrey was at work on the north side of Arch Street. He furthermore states that he derived his knowledge of the incident, which was authentic, from an intimate of Godfrey's, his own grandfather, who lived to be 108 years old.

[1] In the *American Magazine* for July and August, 1758, the "Authors" made a genuine effort to do justice to Godfrey's memory, printing his letter to the Royal Society, as well as Logan's two letters. *Cf.* also, Armistead's "Memoir of Logan."

Scholars of the stamp of David Rittenhouse, of Philadelphia, and Professor Hutton, of Edinburgh, expressed the view that Thomas Godfrey and John Hadley, vice-president of the Royal Society of London, were original inventors of the quadrant, each discovering the principles of the instrument independently of one another. "It was decided that both were entitled to the honor of the invention. . . . The Society sent to Godfrey, as his reward, household furniture to the value of £200. . . ."[1] Godfrey's achievement is embalmed in Barlowe's notices of American men of science in the eighth book of the "Columbiad":

"To guide the sailor in his wandering way,
See Godfrey's glass reverse the beams of day.
His lifted quadrant to the eye displays
From adverse skies the counteracting rays;
And marks, as devious sails bewilder'd roll,
Each nice gradation from the steadfast pole."[2]

In 1743, Godfrey enjoyed the distinction of having his name enrolled as "a mathematician" among the nine original members of the American Philosophical Society, founded by Benjamin Franklin. In 1838, well-nigh a century after his death in 1749, John Fanning Watson, the patriotic annalist of Philadelphia, at his own expense had the remains of Thomas Godfrey, his wife, mother, and father, removed from the burial

[1] Appleton's "Cyclopædia of American Biography", II, 668, 669.

[2] For further confirmation of Godfrey's claim to the invention, compare Miller's "Retrospect of the Eighteenth Century", I, 468–480; the paper by Mr. Walsh, author of "The Appeal"; and Thomas Jefferson's "Notes on Virginia."

ground on the family farm near Germantown, and reinterred in Laurel Hill Cemetery, Philadelphia. The inscription on the old soapstone grave-stones at the family farm were fortunately preserved by Dr. Watson; and are as follows: —

East side: —

Here lyeth the body of JOSEPH, son of Thomas and Frances Godfrey, aged thirty-and-two years, who died the 14th. of 2nd mo. in the year 1705, —
As by grace comes election,
So the end of our hope is resurrection.

West side: —

Death ends man's worke
And labour here.
The man is blest
Whose labour's just and pure.
'Tis vain for man
This life for to adore,
For our dear son
Is dead and gone before;
We hope our Saviour
Him hath justified
Though of his being present
We are now deprived.

Five years later the members of the Philadelphia Commercial Library Company erected a monument, with an appropriate inscription, over the place of Thomas Godfrey's re-interment.[1]

[1] *Cf.* the address of Dr. Emerson, cited above, which was delivered upon the occasion of the dedication of the monument. The inscription on the

III.

"Mr. Godfrey and his father", quaintly observes the poet, Nathaniel Evans, the devoted friend of the former, "may be ranked among the *natural curiosities* of Pennsylvania; for tho' neither of them had much human learning, yet by the peculiar felicity of their natural endowments, each of them were (*sic*) enabled, tho' in different ways, to raise themselves (*sic*) to honor in the learned world."[1] Thomas Godfrey, the younger was born in Philadelphia, on December 4, 1736; and by the death of his father he was left at the age of thirteen to the care of his relatives.

In giving some biographical details of Godfrey, Evans

tombstone, as given in J. F. Watson's "Annals of Philadelphia" (1850 Edition), I, 530, is as follows: —

Here repose the remains
of
Thomas Godfrey
The Inventor of the
Quadrant.
Born 1704, died 1749.
Also,
The remains of his father and mother,
Joseph Godfrey and wife,
They were removed from the
Old homestead by Townsend's first Mill,
October 6, 1838,
By John F. Watson
Viam navitæ complanavit.

Watson says (1850) that "There has since been a monument placed there", to mark the spot where Thomas Godfrey, the inventor, was originally interred. See also Scharf and Wescott's "History of Philadelphia."

[1] Preface to "Juvenile Poems on Various Subjects" etc., Phila., 1765. For excellent brief sketches of the Godfreys, father and son, compare "The Lives of Eminent Philadelphians now Deceased", by Henry Simpson. Philadelphia, 1859.

Monument to Thomas Godfrey, Senior
Laurel Hill Cemetery, Philadelphia

states that "he was placed to an English school", and there received "a common education in his mother tongue; and without any other advantage than *that*, a natural genius, and an attentive perusal of the works of our English Poets, he soon exhibited to the world the strongest proofs of poetical capacity."

A question of no little interest concerns the identity of this "English school" which young Godfrey attended in Philadelphia. Benjamin West, who afterwards won international fame as a painter, was the means of bringing together Godfrey and the man who proved so benevolent a patron, William Smith. "The Academy and Charitable School of Philadelphia", the earliest erected of all the buildings of the later University of Pennsylvania, had as its first President, Benjamin Franklin, who was elected November 13, 1749. The institution opened its doors to students on January 7, 1751. William Smith, a graduate of the University of Aberdeen, began teaching at the Academy on May 29, 1754; and the next year he was chosen Provost of the institution, which was then given the new title of "The College, Academy and Charitable School of Philadelphia in the Province of Pennsylvania." Meeting Benjamin West, who was born October 10, 1738, in West's fifteenth year at Lancaster and perceiving that his education was being neglected, Smith suggested to the elder West to "send his son to the Capital" where he, Smith, "kindly proposed to direct his studies." John Galt, West's biographer, in speaking of West's boyhood days in Philadelphia, records: "Provost Smith introduced West, among other persons, to four young men, pupils of his own, whom he particularly recommended to his acquaintance, as possessing endowments of mind greatly superior to the common standard" — especially referring to Francis Hopkinson, who as he says "afterwards highly distinguished himself in the early proceedings of the Congress of the United States", and Thomas Godfrey, who "died after having given the most promising indications of an elegant genius for pathetic and descriptive poetry." [1] Godfrey was apprenticed to a watchmaker, believed to have been Daniel Evans, a relative and probably the father, of Godfrey's intimate friend, Nathaniel Evans, himself a poet of real promise.[2] It seems clear, then, that Godfrey was one of Smith's pupils, in the College, the Academy, or the Charitable School.

It was during this apprenticeship to the watchmaker, presumably Daniel Evans, that young Godfrey "secretly wrote a poem, which he published anonymously in the Philadelphia newspaper, under the title of 'The Temple of Fame.'" [3] "The attention which it attracted", observes Galt, "induced West, who was in the poet's confidence, to mention to him (Provost Smith) who was the author. The information excited the alert benevolence of Smith's character. . . ." In the extended biography of Smith, it is stated that Smith "encouraged Godfrey to cultivate his abilities, and not only supplied him with much valuable information, but also introduced him to the society of a number of his students, already endeared to him by

[1] "The Life and Studies of Benjamin West." Philadelphia: 1816.

[2] *Cf.* Joseph Jackson: *Public Ledger,* Phila., March 21, 1915.

[3] Galt's "West." This poem is not included in Godfrey's collected works.

their excellent disposition and accomplishments." [1] This account clearly disagrees with the account given by Galt; but as Galt's book is practically an autobiography of Benjamin West and was published sixty years earlier, it is accepted as giving the true account. The lists of the students of the Academy are not complete; and so it is not possible to corroborate from that source the supposition, amounting almost to a certainty, that Godfrey was a pupil at the institution of which Smith was Provost. Although Thomas Godfrey, the elder, as demonstrated by J. F. Watson, was neither poor nor uneducated, he was undoubtedly a man of quite limited means; and it seems not improbable that Thomas Godfrey the younger attended the "Charitable School" connected with the institution. Upon discovering the identity of the author of "The Temple of Fame", Smith exhibited the "alert benevolence" of his character by losing no time "until he had procured the release of Godfrey from his indenture, and a respectable employment for him in the service of the State. . . ."

The young men, of "excellent disposition and accomplishments", with whom young Godfrey was thus thrown in Philadelphia were Benjamin West, whose genius for painting subsequently won him world-wide fame; Francis Hopkinson, in later days talented writer and author of "The Battle of the Kegs"; Jacob Duché, who afterwards was Rector of St. Peter's Church, Philadelphia, and first Chaplain of Congress; [2]

[1] "Life and Correspondence of the Rev. William Smith, D. D.", by his great grandson, Horace Wemyss Smith. Philadelphia, 1879, I, 389–391.

[2] Account of Thomas Godfrey, the poet, written by Richard Penn Smith,

Joseph Reed, aide-de-camp and military secretary to Washington in 1775; John Green, a forgotten portrait painter; and Nathaniel Evans, a brother poet, who after Godfrey's death collaborated with Provost Smith in bringing out an edition of Godfrey's poetical works.

"When very young", says William Smith in regard to Godfrey, "he discovered a strong inclination to Painting, and was very desirous of being bred to that profession. But those who had the charge of him, not having the same honorable idea either of the profession or its utility which he had, crossed him in that desire; which affected him so nearly that it made him contract a sort of melancholy air, and choose to be much by himself; which was considered by many as sourness of temper and want of spirit. . . . Every moment he could be absent from his business was employed in reading and writing, or in the company of a young gentleman a Painter in this place, who was his sole acquaintance and friend." This "young gentleman a Painter" who was certainly not Godfrey's *sole* acquaintance and friend, was none other than John Green; for in a foot-note in the published works of Godfrey, on page 39, we read: "Mr. John Green, an ingenious Portrait-Painter, a particular friend of Mr. Godfrey's, and Author of the Elegy, that precedes these Poems, on Mr. G.'s death." In his poem, "A Night-Piece", Godfrey naïvely pays the following equivocal com-

son of Provost William Smith. The supposition that the younger Godfrey attended the Charitable School is strengthened by the statement of H. W. Smith, who says: "Godfrey, the father . . . was very poor, and could do nothing for his son." *Cf.* "Life and Correspondence of the Rev. William Smith, D. D.", I, 187, 389–391.

pliment, doubtless intended to be sincere, to the art of his friend, who is thus seen to have been a landscapist as well as a portrait-painter: —

"What hand can picture forth the solemn scene,
The deepening shade and the faint glimm'ring light!
How much above th' expressive art of G——n
Are the dim beauties of the dewy night."

Something of the intimacy between Godfrey and Reed is revealed by Galt in his biography of West. Many of Godfrey's verses, we are told, "were composed under a clump of pines, which grew near the upper ferry of the Schuylkill, to which spot he sometimes accompanied West and their mutual friend to angle. In the heat of the day he used to stretch himself beneath the shade of the trees, and repeat to them his verses as he composed them. Reid was the name of the other young man, and the same person who first opposed the British troops in their passing through Jersey, when the rebellion of the provinces commenced." The person here referred to, whose name is misspelled, was, as we know, Joseph Reed (1741–1785), afterwards delegate in the Continental Congress (1777–1778), one of the founders of the University of Pennsylvania, and distinguished in many other capacities.[1] That poem of Godfrey's which we can definitely associate with the Schuylkill River is dedicated "To Mr. N. E." — Nathaniel Evans, undoubtedly; and the first lines of this "Cantata on Peace, 1763" read as follows: —

[1] *Cf.* "Life and Correspondence of Joseph Reed." By Wm. B. Reed, 2 vols., Phila., 1847. Also "Illustrated American Biography", N. Y., 1853, II., 119–120.

Where *Schuylkil's* banks the shades adorn,
    And roses op'ning to the morn,
    Give odours to the breeze;
Thus *Corydon*, a tuneful Swain,
Tun'd his soft reed a soothing strain,
    By Nature form'd to please.

IV.

The bonds of intimacy connecting this group of young men are of sufficient interest to be put in evidence. Among the founders of the Philadelphia Academy who signed the Constitution on Nov. 13, 1749, were Benjamin Franklin, the first President, a fellow-member with Thomas Godfrey, Senior, of the American Philosophical Society, and James Logan, Godfrey's zealous patron. Another one of the original trustees was Thomas Hopkinson, father of Francis Hopkinson, young Godfrey's friend; and another of Godfrey's friends, Jacob Duché, married the sister of his class-mate, Francis Hopkinson. The first graduates of "The College, Academy and Charitable School of Philadelphia" at the Commencement, which was held in College Hall on May 17, 1757, were Jacob Duché, Francis Hopkinson, James Latta, Samuel Magaw, John Morgan, and Hugh Williamson. This Hugh Williamson, born in 1735, was doubtless one of young Godfrey's acquaintances; for he was a tutor in mathematics at the Academy from 1756 to 1758; and it is perhaps worthy of record also that Jacob Duché was made Professor of Oratory in the College of Philadelphia two years after graduation, and held that position for nineteen years. Like young Godfrey,

The Academy and Charitable School of Philadelphia
From the painting by C. M. Leffert

Hugh Williamson was afterwards intimately associated with the life and history of North Carolina, whither he removed about 1777. Williamson wrote the first history of North Carolina, was a member of the Continental Congress from N. C. (1782–1785, 1787–1788), and delegate respectively to the Annapolis Convention (1786) and to the General Convention (1787) which formed the Constitution of the United States.

The affectionate mutual interest of the members of this intimate group is still further illustrated in the tribute which they paid each other in the media of their respective arts. West painted the portrait of Provost Smith, which is still preserved; [1] and also a portrait of Thomas Godfrey, Jr., which careful search has thus far failed to bring to light.[2] In the Historical Society's collection there is, according to Joseph Jackson, "a book of youthful sketches by West, without date, but obviously of this (youthful) period, in which there is a portrait of Green, and several unidentified portraits, one of them believed to be of Godfrey." [3] The deep regard and tender sentiment, not unmixed with sincere admiration, which Green cherished for Godfrey is well expressed in his "Elegy, To the Memory of Mr. Thomas Godfrey", with the Horatian motto:—

[1] "University of Pennsylvania", by E. P. Cheyney and E. P. Oberholtzer. Boston: R. Herndon Co., I, 63.

[2] In the biography of Provost Smith, Richard Penn Smith says: "There was long in my father's possession a portrait by West of his young friend." It is to be feared that this portrait was not a flattering likeness — neither good art nor good portraiture; for Seilhamer quotes from some source the statement that this portrait was "indicative of talent neither in the artist nor the person delineated."

[3] *Public Ledger*, March 21, 1915.

Quis desiderio fit pudor aut modus
Tam chari capitis?

which occupies the leading place in the edition of Godfrey's works edited by Nathaniel Evans. In this same edition, to which Provost Smith anonymously contributed an elaborate critical postscript, appears Evans' "Elegy, to the Memory of the same", with date, Oct. 1, 1763 — two months after Godfrey's death.[1] Among a very extended list of subscribers, we note with interest, from the small group in which our interest particularly centers, the following: Benjamin Franklin, Esq., LL. D., F. R. S., who subscribed for twelve copies; Rev[d]. William Smith, D. D., Provost of the College and Academy of Philadelphia, who subscribed for four copies; Rev[d]. Jacob Duché, A. M., one of the assistant ministers of Christ Church and St. Peter's, who subscribed for two copies; Hon. Col. Henry Bouquet, under whom Godfrey had served in the campaign against Fort Duquesne in 1758; and Godfrey's close and familiar friend, the painter John Green.

Nathaniel Evans was not graduated with his own class at the Philadelphia Academy, whither he was sent "soon after it was first opened, and before the collegiate part of the Institution was begun." It is stated by Provost Smith that "his parents, who were reputable citizens, designing him for merchandize, put him Apprentice"; and shortly after finishing his ap-

[1] "Juvenile Poems on Various Subjects, with The Prince of Parthia, a Tragedy. To which is prefixed some Account of the Author and his Writings." Philadelphia, Henry Miller, 1765.

prenticeship, he "returned to the College, and applied himself, with great diligence, to the study of Philosophy and the Sciences, till the Commencement, May 30, 1765; when on account of his great merit and promising genius, he was, by special Mandate of the Trustees, upon the recommendation of the Provost and Faculty of Professors, complimented with a Diploma for the degree of Master of Arts; although he had not taken the previous degree of Bachelor of Arts, on account of the interruption in his course of studies, during the term of his apprenticeship." Immediately after the Commencement, he embarked for England and was admitted into holy orders by the Lord Bishop of London, Dr. Terrick. He was appointed by the Society for the Propagation of the Gospel in Foreign Parts to the new Mission for Gloucester County, N. J. Upon his return from England at the end of 1765, he immediately undertook the work of the Mission; but lived just long enough (Oct. 29, 1767), says Smith, "to show, by the goodness of his temper, the purity of his morals, the cheerfulness and affability of his conversation, the sublimity and soundness of his doctrines, and the warmth of his Pulpit Composition, how well he was qualified for the sacred office, to which he had now wholly devoted himself."

Shortly after Evans' death, Provost Smith filled for him the same office of literary executor which Evans, with his expert assistance, had a few years before filled for Godfrey. Owing to numerous interruptions, of which he speaks in the Introduction, he was unable to bring out this edition of Evans' poems until 1772 — his introduction bearing at the end the inscription

"Philadelphia, August 1, 1772." [1] Among subscribers to this work, it is interesting to note the names of Oliver Goldsmith, Esq., London, and of Evans' old friend of Academy days, now Reverend Jacob Duché, A. M., Assistant Minister of Christ Church and St. Peter's, Philadelphia, and Chaplain to the Right Hon. the Earl of Stirling — who subscribed for two copies.

V.

In May, 1758, Provost Smith procured from the Governor of Pennsylvania a commission as ensign for his protégé, Godfrey.[2] At the age of twenty-two, Godfrey joined the Pennsylvania forces then being raised for an expedition against Fort Duquesne, and served during the course of the campaign. In his "Poetical Essays", in the *American Magazine*, of September, 1758, Provost Smith states that it was Godfrey's "lot and mortification to be left in garrison at one of our out-forts, when his great desire would be the scene of action, and to sing those victories and triumphs, which, 'tis hoped, we shall yet reap."

During the second quarter of the century, North Carolina became a Mecca for the migratory population

[1] "Poems on Several Occasions, with Some Other Compositions", by Nathaniel Evans, A. M. Phila., John Dunlap, 1772.

[2] "Pennsylvania Archives", II, 131. He was undoubtedly recommended by Provost Smith for a lieutenant's commission, as mentioned in H. W. Smith's biography of Provost Smith; but no official record of Godfrey's commission as lieutenant has been found. He was probably given that rank after the campaign was under way; for it is categorically stated by his intimate friend, Evans, in the following foot-note to the "Epistle to a Friend from Fort Henry", dated August 10, 1758: "Wrote, when the Author was a Lieutenant in the Pennsylvania Forces, and garrisoned at Fort Henry."

of Pennsylvania; and doubtless Thomas Godfrey, the elder, had read in the *Pennsylvania Gazette*, edited by his friend and fellow-scientist, Benjamin Franklin, the letters from North Carolina, written by Franklin's former partner, Hugh Meredith. These elaborate and roseate pictures of North Carolina which, as Franklin remarks, "gave great satisfaction to the publick", may very well have proved mildly alluring to young Godfrey. But his immediate interest in North Carolina was most probably aroused as the result of being thrown into association with the famous North Carolina rangers, during the course of the campaign against Fort Duquesne, and with their popular commander, expert in Indian and border warfare, under whom Daniel Boone had formerly served, Major Hugh Waddell, of Wilmington. Indeed it was not long after his return to Philadelphia, in the late winter of 1758–1759, that he was offered a situation as factor in Wilmington — presumably at the instance of his brother officer, Hugh Waddell, impressed by his personality and talents. In the spring of 1759 he embarked for Wilmington, which he was to find conspicuous alike for the literary culture of its leading citizens and the gayety of the social life.

VI.

The village of New Town, facing the Cape Fear River, was laid off as early as April, 1733. Five years before this, North Carolina had been divided into three counties, Albemarle, Bath, and Clarendon. The last named "had but one precinct, styled New Hanover, embracing the settlements on both sides of the lower Cape Fear, and numbering a population of about five hundred." In his admirable "Description", McRee says: "To the Florist and Botanist no section of the globe, of equal extent, is more deeply interesting than the immediate neighborhood of Wilmington. A never ending and varied beauty, follows the seasons. Festoons of the virgins-bower and clustering grape; pleasant savannahs, enamelled with blossoms of every hue, and rivalling the richest gardens of the old world; the tulip-tree, the live oak; the cypress and juniper; and the dionea, spreading its snare for the thoughtless fly, form a scene of enchantment on every side, encircling the glistening white sands of the Town with a girdle of unfading verdure."

In 1736 the site of the present Wilmington was occupied as a trading post by a few merchants; but it was not until 1739 that the settlement known as Newton was established by law as a town. The name of Wilmington was bestowed upon the town by Governor Gabriel Johnston as a compliment to his patron, to whose kind offices he was indebted for his position, Sir Spencer Compton, Earl of Wilmington, a nobleman of ability and distinction, who for many years had occupied a high position at court, and was soon to become Prime Minister.

As affording a little glimpse of conditions on the Cape Fear at this period, a quotation may be given from a letter written from Wilmington, in 1741, by James Murray, of London, one of the Governor's Council: "In my home there is a large room 22 × 16 feet the most airy of any in the country, two tolerable lodging rooms and a closet upstairs and garrets above. A cellar below divided into a kitchen with an oven and a store for liquors, provisions &c. this makes one half of any house. The other, placed on the east end, is the store cellar below, the store and counting house on the first floor and above it is partitioned off into four rooms, but this end is side plaistered, but only done with rough boards."[1] In the act of incorporation of the town, it was enacted "that no person should be deemed qualified to be a Representative of said town to sit in the General Assembly, unless he was seizin of a brick, stone or frame house with one or more chimneys", the house to be at least thirty feet long and sixteen feet wide. In an unpublished letter to the young Samuel Johnston, Junior, afterwards the distinguished North Carolina statesman of that name, written from Wilmington little more than a year before the arrival of Thomas Godfrey, Peter du Bois gives a graphic picture of the town and its development. Comparing it with New Bern, another town in eastern North Carolina, long known as "the Athens of North Carolina", he says: "I confess the spot on which its built is not so Level nor so good a Soil, But the Regularity of the Streets are (*sic*) equal to those (*sic*) of Philadelph^a and the Buildings in General very Good. Many of Brick, two or three Stories High with double Piazas wch. make a good appear^ce."[2] A brief period only for the cultivation of better acquaintance with the inhabitants is doubtless all that is required to enable the convivial du Bois to realize the true spirit of the place; for he continues: "I cannot yet find a Social C°. who will Drink Claret & Smoke Tobacco

[1] "Letters of a Loyalist."

[2] "Archives, North Carolina Historical Commission", Raleigh, N. C.

till four in the morning. I hope however to make some proselytes soon. In which very Righteous attempt I don't doubt but shall have the best wishes of all Lovers of Society, among the Numbers of wch. I do not omit to count Mr. Johnston."

True "lovers of Society" were indeed to be found in this town of Wilmington, noted afar for its lavish hospitality and the polite learning of its inhabitants. After 1740, as Wheeler, the historian of North Carolina, records, it was the custom of the people of the Cape Fear section to send their sons to Harvard, while the inhabitants of the northeastern counties sent their sons to the universities of Great Britain. In the language of the gifted annalist, McRee, men of rare talents, fortune, and attainment united to render Wilmington "the home of politeness, and ease, and enjoyment." It was with this society — with women of wit and men educated at the great universities — that young Thomas Godfrey, of brilliant talents yet humble origin, came to mingle during his sojourn in Wilmington.

This section of North Carolina was described by the Royal Governor, Josiah Martin, as "the region of politeness and hospitality"; and the literary taste of the inhabitants is exemplified in the public and private libraries of this region, notably the "Cape Fear Library", supported by a society of gentlemen, and the private library of Samuel Johnston, a quarter of a century later numbering upwards of five thousand volumes. "Festive entertainment, balls, every species of amusement which song and dance could afford", says Archibald Maclaine Hooper, a younger contemporary, "were resorted to. The neighing courser and the echoing horn, the sports of the turf and the pleasure of the chase, were alternately the objects of eager pursuit. . . . This general ease and prosperity was highly favorable to the cultivation of polite literature. . . . Every family possessed a collection of the best English authors. . . . Wit and humor, music and poetry, were drawn into action in social and convivial intercourse. Conversation was cultivated to a high degree."[1] The biographer of Associate Justice Iredell, of the U. S. Supreme Court, remarks of Wilmington that "the higher civilization of the Old World had been transplanted there, and had taken vigorous root."[2]

Conspicuous members of this patrician society were John Ashe, afterwards General in the Revolution, "the very Rupert of debate"; Cornelius Harnett, "the pride of the Cape Fear", the famous patriot described by Josiah Quincy as the "Samuel Adams of North Carolina", who could "boast a genius for music and taste for letters"; Samuel Ashe, afterwards Governor of the State; Dr. John Eustace, the correspondent of Sterne, a gentleman who "united wit and genius, learning and science"; Col. Thomas Lloyd, a master of classical learning; Dr. John Fergus, "of stately presence, with velvet coat, cocked hat, and gold headed cane, graduate of Edinburgh"; William Pennington, afterwards Master of the Ceremonies at Bath, "an elegant writer, admired for his wit, and his highly polished urbanity"; Archibald Maclaine, "whose criticisms on Shakespeare would, if they were pub-

[1] *N. C. Univ. Magazine,* June, 1860.

[2] "Life and Correspondence of James Iredell", in 2 vols. By Griffith J. McRee.

lished, give him fame and rank in the republic of letters"; William Hill, graduate of Harvard, praised by Quincy for his exquisite politeness; Lewis Henry de Rosset, a "cultivated and elegant gentleman", whose titled ancestors were signally honored by the Grand Monarque; Maurice Moore, afterwards distinguished as judge, a brilliant pamphleteer — "as a wit, always prompt in reply; as an orator, always 'daring the mercy of chance'"; and others little less distinguished. "No better society existed in America", says the biographer of Hugh Waddell, "and it is but simple truth to say that for classical learning, wit, oratory, and varied accomplishments no generation of their successors has equalled them." [1]

After Godfrey left Philadelphia upon the voyage which finally landed him safely as commission merchant at Wilmington, his devoted friend, Nathaniel Evans, addressed to him a sprightly "Ode — Attempted in the manner of Horace",[2] in which he touches upon the subjects of their mutual concern: their poetic aspirations, their enforced engagement in uncongenial pursuits, and their desire to devote their best energies and talents to literature. The first two stanzas, we may observe, vividly project the picture of Godfrey on his way to North Carolina.

[1] "A Colonial Officer and his Times", by Alfred Moore Waddell.

[2] "Poems on Several Occasions, with Some Other Compositions." Phila., John Dunlap, 1772. In a foot-note to this poem, dedicated "To my Ingenious Friend, Mr. Thomas Godfrey", one reads, "Mr. Evans and he were intimate in *life* and in *death* not long divided. They possessed a kind of congenial spirits, and their fates were not dissimilar. Both courted the Muses from their very infancy; and both were called from this world as they were but entering into their state of manhood."

While you, dear Tom, are forc'd to roam,
In search of fortune, far from home,
O'er bogs, o'er seas and mountains;
I too, debar'd the soft retreat
Of shady groves, and murmur sweet
Of silver-prattling fountains,

Must mingle with the bustling throng,
And bear my load of cares along,
Like any other sinner:
For, where's the ecstacy in this,
To loiter in poetic bliss,
And go without a dinner?

Flaccus, we know, immortal bard!
With mighty kings and statesmen far'd,
And lived in cheerful plenty:
But now, in these degenerate days,
The slight reward of empty praise,
Scarce one receives in twenty.

Well might the Roman swan, along
The pleasing Tiber, pour his song,
When blest with ease and quiet;
Oft did he grace Mæcenas' board,
Who would for him throw by the lord,
And in Falernian riot.

But dearest Tom! these days are past,
And we are in a climate cast
Where few the Muse can relish;
Where all the doctrine now that's told,

Is that a shining heap of gold
Alone can man embellish.

Then since 'tis thus, my honest friend,
If you be wise, my strain attend,
And counsel sage adhere to;
With me, henceforward, join the crowd,
And like the rest proclaim aloud,
That MONEY is all VIRTUE.

Then may we both, in time, retreat,
To some fair villa, sweetly neat,
To entertain the Muses;
And then life's noise and troubles leave —
Supremely blest, we'll never grieve
At what the world refuses.

In the gracious and courtly society of Wilmington, young Godfrey, whom his friend Evans described as a "man of lovely character", was surely not "debarred the soft retreat of shady groves, and murmur sweet of silver-prattling fountains", even though his trade as factor compelled him to "mingle with the bustling throng", and bear his "load of cares along." He no doubt keenly enjoyed his association with the Shakespearean and classical scholars of the Cape Fear — with Fergus, Moore, Maclaine, and Eustace. And these, in their turn, welcomed into their inner circle the budding young poet, and encouraged him in his literary aspirations. Friendship was the natural atmosphere of this young poet of whom his biographer could truly say: "His sweet, amiable disposition, his integrity of heart, his engaging modesty and diffidence of manner,

AN

ODE

Attempted in the Manner of HORACE,

TO MY INGENIOUS FRIEND,

MR. *THOMAS GODFREY.

I.

WHILE you, dear TOM, are forc'd to roam,
In search of fortune, far from home,
O'er bogs, o'er seas and mountains;
I too, debar'd the soft retreat
Of shady groves, and murmur sweet
Of silver-prattling fountains,

II. Must

* See an account of the THOMAS GODFREYS, father and son, in the American Magazine. The above little ode is addressed to the son. Mr. *Evans* and he were intimate in *life*, and in *death* not long divided. They possessed a kind of congenial spirits, and their fates were not dissimilar. Both courted the Muses from their very infancy; and both were called from this world as they were but entering into their state of manhood. On Mr. Godfrey's death, Mr. *Evans* collected and published his pieces in a small volume, and soon afterwards left his *own* pieces to the like friendly care of others.

FACSIMILE OF EVANS' ODE TO GODFREY
First page

his fervent and disinterested love of his friends, endeared him to all those who shared his acquaintance, and stamped the image of him in indelible characters on the hearts of his more intimate friends." [1]

In Wilmington, young Godfrey, the congenial companion and loyal friend, was soon on friendly, and even intimate, terms with all classes of the people, from the Provincial Secretary and the Commander of the Fort to the town engineer and the sheriff of the County. The summer colony of the most distinguished figures of the day was located on Masonborough Sound, some seven miles below Wilmington, thus named because a number of zealous Masons originally built there, so closely together, as to create a straggling village, or hamlet; and here Godfrey formed the acquaintance, and doubtless won the friendship as well, of Cornelius Harnett, afterwards to become the great revolutionary leader of North Carolina; Col. Alexander Lillington, afterwards General and hero of the decisive battle of Moore's Creek Bridge; and Archibald Maclaine, the able lawyer and refined Shakespearean scholar. "Godfrey spent his summers at Masonboro Sound", relates the distinguished antiquarian, Colonel James Green Burr, "and was highly esteemed for his many good qualities. He wrote a piece upon Masonboro and many others of local interest, which survived for years in the recollection of the people of this section but which have long since been forgotten." [2] In the appendix to the *Life and Correspondence of James Ire-*

[1] Preface to Godfrey's "Poetical Works."

[2] "Early History of the Lower Cape Fear": *James Sprunt Historical Monograph*, IV, 126. University of North Carolina Press. 1904.

dell, McRee records that "many of the minor pieces in his (Godfrey's) collection of poems, abound in local allusions." Among these may be especially singled out for mention the "Epistle to a Friend", dated August 10, 1758, and written while the author was garrisoned at Fort Henry: "To the Memory of General Wolfe"; and "Victory", his last published poem, which appeared in the *Pennsylvania Gazette* and celebrated the success of the British arms in America. In his "History of the Town of Wilmington", published in the *Wilmington Chronicle*, Sept. 16, 1846, McRee further states: "He (Godfrey) was much of a reader, — well versed in the English poets, and was himself a poet of no mean rank. He wrote several pieces descriptive of the locality where he dwelt. One was on Masonboro Sound and possessed great beauty, being remarkable for its felicity of diction and thought, and its graphic excellence. . . . The verses of this poet were once greatly in vogue in the neighborhood in which he had selected a home, and found friends warm and steady; and there were but few gentlemen who could not repeat from memory some passages from his pen. His works were published, but no copy can now be found where his genius was fostered and first put forth its tender leaves."

Fortunately, the "piece upon Masonboro" has been preserved; and leads us to believe that Godfrey not only wooed the Muses at Masonboro, but also lost his heart there, mayhap one summer night, along the moonlit sound. In a foot-note, "Masonborough" is described as a "pleasant Retreat, nigh Cape Fear, in North Carolina."

On Masonboro Sound

The environment in which The Prince of Parthia was written

O Come to Masonborough's grove,
  Ye Nymphs and Swains away,
Where blooming Innocence and Love,
  And Pleasure crown the day.

Here dwells the Muse, here her bright Seat
  Erects the lovely Maid,
From Noise and Show, a blest retreat,
  She seeks the sylvan shade.

Hence Myra, with that scornful air,
  Nor frown within this grove,
Fell hate shall find no resting here,
  'Tis sacred all to Love.

And Chloe, on whose wanton breast
  Lascivious breezes play,
'Tis Innocence that makes us blest,
  And as the Season gay.

Ye noisy Revellers retire,
  Bear your loud laughter hence,
'Tis Virtue shall our Songs inspire,
  And Mirth without offense.

The Queen of Beauty, all divine,
  Here spreads her gentle reign,
See, all around, the graces shine,
  Like Cynthia's silver train.

VII.

During the period of his residence in North Carolina, Godfrey evidently visited various towns in the eastern part of the Colony — Edenton, New Bern, Brunswick, and Cross Creek (now Fayetteville). Among his friends and acquaintances were Colonel Benjamin Heron, Esq., Provincial Secretary; William Bartram, the famous botanist and traveller; Obadiah Holt, the sheriff of New Hanover County; Colonel James Moore, commander of Fort Johnson near the mouth of the Cape Fear, and afterwards General in the Revolution; Colonel Caleb Grainger, one of the first eight aldermen of the town of Wilmington, elected in 1760; Judge Alexander Martin, of Cross Creek, afterwards famous as Governor of North Carolina; Mrs. Anne Nessfield, whose daughter married the famous Federalist, the friend of Washington, Adams, and Jefferson, General John Steele; Colonel William Purviance, active patriot and member of the Committee of Safety; Robert Schaw, Colonel of Artillery under Governor Tryon in the expedition against the Regulators in 1771; William Davis, afterwards Major in the Revolution; and Alexander Duncan, town engineer of Wilmington.[1]

A fragment of documentary evidence, negative though it be, gives one an amused, albeit faint, glimpse of Godfrey through the obscurity of the period. One of the early laws of Wilmington compelled all the taxables, several times each year, together with the

[1] These names are taken from the list of subscribers for the edition of Godfrey's works edited by Nathaniel Evans in 1765. It is presumed that those who, in remote Carolina, subscribed to a book of poems published in Philadelphia two years after the death of the author, must have had the strong reasons of friendship and acquaintance to induce them to subscribe. Other names of subscribers from North Carolina are James Bailey, William Campell, Alexander Chapman, Robert Cohren (Cochrane), Walter Dubois, Cornelius Harnett, Robert Johnson, Archibald McDuffei, Archibald Maclaine, John Robeson, Patrick Stewart, James Stewart, and William Watkins.

able-bodied men of the town, black and white, to work from three to six days at a time on the streets and wharves, and on the road from Pt. Peter to Mt. Misery. Usually, there was a long list of delinquents, who failed to answer the call. In July, 1760, for some strange reason, virtually the entire population of Wilmington must have "turned out"; for the list of defaulters, as given in the county records, was singularly brief, numbering only twenty in all. Among these delinquents in civic duty was the young poet, Thomas Godfrey, mayhap busy at the time upon *The Court of Fancy*, his long poem modelled on Chaucer's *House of Fame*. Who, indeed, we may well inquire, would expect of a dreamy poet devotion to such prosaic social service as road upkeep a century and a half in advance of the age? Thomas Godfrey, like many of us, cared more for poems than for picks, for spondees than for spontoons. Perhaps, thus early, he already had rapt visions of the quiet wooing of the muses, seductively depicted by his friend Evans in his playful ode: —

"Then may we both, in time, retreat,
To some fair villa, sweetly neat,
To entertain the Muses;
And then life's noise and trouble leave —
Supremely blest, we'll never grieve
At what the world refuses." [1]

During his sojourn of three years in North Carolina, Godfrey often contributed verse to the *American Magazine* of Philadelphia, edited by his friend and patron, William Smith. Certain of these poems were

[1] "Poems on Several Occasions", 50–52.

published in the *Monthly Review* of London; and the "authors" of that review stated of Godfrey: "He certainly has *genius;* and we are sorry he had not education to improve it." The chief preoccupation of his fancy when he first arrived in North Carolina, however, was a stage-play which he was engaged in writing. In the Philadelphia society of this period, there was a deep interest in plays and in the drama generally. Favorite authors for discussion — their invention, style, imagery, diction — were Addison, Prior, Congreve, Dryden, Pope, and Shakespeare.[1] At the age of thirteen, Godfrey might have seen produced at Plumstead's, by the Murray and Kean players, in August, 1749, Addison's *Cato*, a play which manifestly influenced him in the choice of subject and setting for his own tragedy.[2] It is possible that during the same year he may have seen the same company's productions of Otway's *Orphan* and Shakespeare's *Richard III.* Plays in Hallam's repertory which doubtless exerted some influence upon Godfrey in the writing of his own stage-piece, plays which he may have seen produced (April 15 to June 12, 1754), are Shakespeare's *Romeo and Juliet*, Farquhar's *Tamerlane*, and Rowe's *Tamerlane.* It is most probable that

[1] "Journal of William Black." Cited in O. Seilhamer: "History of the American Theatre", I, 195.

[2] *Cf.* Journal of John Smith, who was a nephew of James Logan, in the following entry: —

Sixth Month (August) 22, 1749. Joseph Morris and I happened in at Peacock Bigger's, and drunk tea there, and his daughter, being one of the company who were going to hear the tragedy of *Cato* acted, it occasioned some conversation, in which I expressed my sorrow that anything of the kind was encouraged.

Godfrey was present on June 19, 1754, when Hallam and his company produced Cibber's *Careless Husband* and the farce, *Harlequin Collector*, the proceeds going "for the benefit of the charity children belonging to the Academy in this City." [1]

Certain it is that when David Douglas, who had been united in marriage to the widow of the elder Lewis Hallam, the actor, brought his company to Philadelphia in the spring of 1759, the news soon reached Godfrey in Wilmington, and animated him to feverish efforts to complete his tragedy in time to have it produced by Douglas' company in Philadelphia. His leisure hours during the summer and autumn of 1759 he devoted to the hurried completion of "The Prince of Parthia." The last act, which he left in a somewhat unfinished state, evidences his haste. It must not be forgotten, in any consideration of Godfrey as a dramatist, that "The Prince of Parthia" was not designed as a mere closet-drama, but was written with the avowed object of stage-production. "As he knew the Company (Douglas' Company) was about to break up", comments Provost Smith, in the "Postscript" to Evans' edition of Godfrey's poetical works, "and he might not soon have another opportunity of trying his success this way, he was willing to offer it." Fortunately, the fragment of a letter dated November 17, 1759, has come down to us, written from Wilmington by Godfrey to a friend in Philadelphia, doubtless Provost Smith: "By the last

[1] *Pennsylvania Gazette*, Jan. 20, 1754. There are good grounds, as we have seen, for the belief that, at this time, Godfrey was a pupil at the charity school connected with the Philadelphia Academy.

vessel from this place, I sent you the copy of a Tragedy I finished here, and desired your interest in bringing it on the stage; I have not yet heard of the vessel's arrival, and believe if she is safe, it will be too late for the company now in Philadelphia." In view of the unfinished state of the manuscript, "nothing but that fondness which every Author has for a performance when it comes first from his pen," observes Smith with quiet humor, "would have made him propose it for the stage." Godfrey's surmise, that his manuscript would reach Philadelphia too late for the production of his tragedy by Hallam's Company at this time, proved well founded. The letter mentioned above did not reach Philadelphia until after the arrival there of the manuscript of "The Prince of Parthia." Douglas's Company completed its season on December 27, 1759; it was not to return to Philadelphia until November, 1766, when the Southwark, which has been described as the "first permanent theatre on this continent", was opened.

Upon the death of his employer, Godfrey left Wilmington and returned to Philadelphia. No opening in business immediately presenting itself there, he procured some small commissions and sailed as a supercargo to the Island of New Providence. Returning by water in the early summer of 1763 to Wilmington, to which he was now endeared by many happy associations, he might perhaps have written there a great poetic drama, foreshadowed by the budding genius displayed in "The Prince of Parthia" had not death suddenly singled him out. "It is with infinite regret I inform you", reads an "Extract of a

Letter from a Gentleman in Wilmington, North Carolina",[1] "that he, whom I esteemed one of the worthiest of Friends (Mr. Thomas Godfrey, of your Place) is no more. Thursday, 25th July, he and myself set out on a small Journey into the Country; the Day being very warm and he not much used to riding, I imagine, overheated him, for the succeeding Night he was seized with a most violent Fever and Vomiting, which desperately increasing, in seven days hurried him out of this mortal life."[2] Thus died at ten o'clock A.M., on the third of August, 1763, at the early age of twenty-six, the poetic and dramatic genius whose name is inextricably linked with North Carolina as the author of "The Prince of Parthia." Not without a peculiar interest in this connection does one read the following lines, inspired by warm admiration and tender sympathy, from the Elegy written by Godfrey's bosom-friend, John Green, the painter, which appears in the collected edition of Godfrey's works:—

Ye gentle Swains of *Carolina's* shore,
Who knew my Damon, (now, alas! no more),
By moon-light round his hallow'd grave repair,
Strew sweetest flow'rs, and drop a sorrowing tear;
With never-fading laurel shade his tomb,
And bid the rising bay forever bloom,
Teach springing flow'rs their purpl'd heads to rise,
And sweetly twining, write, *Here Virtue lies.*
Sing in sad strains each venerable name,

[1] *Pennsylvania Gazette,* Sept. 29, 1763.

[2] Evans describes Godfrey as "of a corpulent habit of body."

In Fortune's spite, that struggl'd up to fame;
By Virtue led life's rugged road along,
Their lives instructive as their sweetest song.
Say, while their praises tremble on the tongue,
Thus liv'd this youthful Bard, thus gentle Damon sung.

VIII.

Thomas Godfrey occupies a significant position in the history of American literature. And this not solely by reason of the fact that he was the author of a single drama which had the unique distinction of being the first tragedy ever written by a native American and produced upon the professional stage in the United States. Wholly unshadowed by the gloomy forebodings of the Puritans, he harks back to the sources of English literature of the Elizabethan and Restoration eras. The publication of his poems in 1765 marks the beginning of a new epoch in American literature; for he was our first conspicuous devotee of the principle of "art for art's sake." Godfrey was a zealous and devoted student of the works of Chaucer, Shakespeare, Spencer, Pope, and Dryden; and his pastorals, love songs, and odes reveal the influence of Waller, Herrick, Wither, and the Cavalier Poets. Unlike the American poets who preceded him, his predilection is for esthetics, rather than ethics; beauty, not morality, is the goddess of his fancy. These juvenile poems addressed to Sylvia, Amyntor, and Chloe, with the loves of Damon, Celia, Thyrsis, Myra, Delia, and Corinna as the subjects of his reflection, not incapably sustain the literary tradition; and they inspire the conviction that had God-

James Logan
After the painting in Independence Hall, Philadelphia

Provost William Smith
After the painting by Gilbert Stuart

frey, who far surpassed in poetic endowment any native American who had preceded him, lived to develop and bring to full fruition his very unusual poetic genius, he would take high rank to-day in the history of American literature.

The Philadelphia society of Godfrey's day was by no means deficient in men of taste, talent, and literary attainment. Pope and Dryden were then the literary dictators of Europe, and exerted a powerful influence in the formation of American literary taste. Yet with the men and women in this Philadelphia society who gave some attention to the study and practice of literature, authors in no way secondary to Pope and Dryden in influence and appeal were Shakespeare, Addison, Otway, Prior, and Congreve. The leading poets of Philadelphia in this period are James Ralph, the friend of Franklin, who wrote many dramas and the bitter attack on Pope, which stung the bard of Twickenham to the familiar couplet; James Logan, versatile and distinguished; Aquila Rose, whose "Poems on Several Occasions" contains the notable lyric, "To his Companion at Sea"; Samuel Keimer, Benjamin Franklin's friend celebrated in the "Autobiography"; George Webbe, the author of "Bachelor's Hall," who shared with Keimer in the publication of the *Pennsylvania Gazette;* Francis Hopkinson, brilliant writer of occasional pieces; Nathaniel Evans, the young clerical, and Provost Smith, author of the remarkable poem on visiting the Academy in Philadelphia in June, 1753 — the last three Godfrey's particular friends. Among lesser luminaries may be mentioned Henry Brooke and Joseph Shippen.

In October, 1757, appeared the first number of the *American Magazine* edited by Dr. William Smith. In January, 1758, a poem entitled "The Invitation" appeared in this magazine, with the following note: "This little poem was sent to us by an unknown hand, and seems dated as an original; if it be so, we think it does honor to our City." In an article in the *American Magazine* of September, 1758, the editor, after speaking in particular of "The Invitation", an "Ode on Friendship", which appeared "in our last magazine", and "The Court of Fancy", then unpublished, observes: "These pieces, and some others of his, fell into our hands by accident, soon after the appearance of the 'Invitation', which was found among the rest; and we reckon it one of the highest instances of good fortune that has befallen us, during the period of our Magazine, that we have had an opportunity of making known to the world so much merit." The "accident" here spoken of was doubtless the discovery, through Benjamin West, of which Galt speaks, that the author of "The Temple of Fame" and "The Invitation" was none other than young Godfrey. The genial provost, as already mentioned, interested himself to procure an ensign's commission for the young poet, and sent him off on the expedition against Fort Duquesne. Godfrey left manuscripts of his poems with one whom Dr. Smith described as "a young gentleman a *Painter* in this place, who was his (Godfrey's) sole acquaintance and friend." While the description would fit either Benjamin West or John Green, it is scarcely open to question, from evidence already detailed, that Godfrey's confidential friend in this instance was Green. In the same article, the "editor" of the *American Magazine* says of Godfrey: "When he went away he left his poetry in the hands of his foresaid friend (Green), by which means we enjoyed that pleasure which his own modesty and diffidence would, perhaps, long have prevented." [1]

Already, Dr. Smith had seen the manuscript of "The Court of Fancy", and in this same article declared that it would, after it had received the author's final corrections, "place him high in the list of *Poets*." The subject he described as one which "none but an elevated and daring genius durst attempt with any degree of success; in managing which, he shines in all the spirit of true *creative Poetry*." This poem, however, did not appear, it seems, and certainly not in book form, until 1762, when it was published in Philadelphia.[2] The next year, in the *Pennsylvania Gazette*, appeared, in the words of Nathaniel Evans, "that nervous and noble song of triumph called *Victory*, which was the last of our Author's pieces that was published."

Among Godfrey's friends at Wilmington, North Carolina, were Archibald Maclaine, the talented Shakespearean scholar, and Cornelius Harnett, a true lover and patron of the arts. It was doubtless one or the other of these two cultured lovers of literature who rescued many of Godfrey's poems for posterity.

[1] This article, entitled "Poetical Essays", pp. 602–603, is followed on p. 604 by Godfrey's "A Pindaric Ode on Wine." In a subsequent issue of this magazine appeared "A Night-Piece", containing the allusion to Godfrey's friend, Green, the painter.

[2] "The Court of Fancy; A Poem." By Thomas Godfrey. Philadelphia: Printed and Sold by William Dunlap. MDCCLXII. 4°, pp. 24.

No doubt the "gentleman in Wilmington" who wrote the letter, an extract from which appeared in the *Pennsylvania Gazette*, of September 29, 1763, announcing the news of Godfrey's death, is the person referred to as follows in Evans' biographical sketch: "The manuscript pieces, therefore, were left in their primitive form, and they fortunately falling into the hands of a Gentleman, a friend of the Author, at the place where he died, were kindly transmitted to this City." From the very time of his death, the expectation was entertained that Godfrey's poems would be published in collected form; for the very issue of the *Pennsylvania Gazette* which contained his obituary also contained the statement that "the Public will be favored with it ('a handsome Octavo Volume') as soon as those pieces which remain in Carolina can be transmitted here." The publication of Godfrey's work was executed with great care; and both Evans and Smith revised the poems, making only such changes as seemed absolutely necessary. Evans himself disclaims credit for originating the idea of making a collection of Godfrey's poems, stating that the "publication was undertaken at the motion, and under the countenance of some Gentlemen here (Philadelphia), of incontestable taste and judgement." Doubtless the prime mover in the matter was Provost Smith; for his grandson, Richard Penn Smith, says that he "collected the various poems of Godfrey, and published them, together with 'The Prince of Parthia', in a volume of 223 quarto pages." [1] Certainly Benjamin

[1] "Life and Correspondence of Rev. William Smith, D.D." By Horace Wemyss Smith, Philadelphia, 1879, I, p. 391. It is inaccurate to say, with-

Reverend Jacob Duché

Joseph Reed

Francis Hopkinson

Hugh Williamson

Franklin was an active patron of the enterprise. The importance of the publication seems to have been recognized by Evans, who bespeaks "the candour of the public in behalf of this collection . . . the first of the kind that this Province has produced."

The songs which Godfrey has left, while somewhat artificial in their attempted grace and lightness, reflect the spirit of the masters he has studied — Waller and Herrick. The song in the opening scene of the fifth act of "The Prince of Parthia" is full of the charm of a picture of Watteau, touched with the insouciant gallantry of the Restoration. Characteristic of this vein is also this dainty trifle: —

When in *Celia's* heav'nly Eye
Soft inviting Love I spy,
Tho' you say 'tis all a cheat,
I must clasp the dear deceit.

Why should I more knowledge gain,
When it only gives me pain?
If deceived I'm still at rest,
In the sweet Delusion blest.

Certain of Godfrey's poems attracted the attention of a foreign public, and won the mild approbation of the editors of the English *Monthly Review*. The poem "Victory" was denominated in this magazine a "pretty Poem"; and the "authors" say of the poet: "Mr. Godfrey possesses a considerable degree of poetical imagination." The opinion in England agreed

out qualification, that he "published" this volume. He wrote the "Post-script", which is anonymous and occupies pp. xiii–xxii.

with that of Godfrey's friends: that he was a genius who needed education, training, and culture in order to develop and fulfil his poetic gifts. His "Epistle to a Friend, from Fort Henry", dated August 10, 1758, and written while he was garrisoned at that post, attracted much attention. Richard Penn Smith refers to it as "a poetic epistle, in which he describes the horrors of savage warfare; the miseries of the frontier inhabitants, and the dreadful carnage of Indian massacres. The description, although agonizing, is given with poetic force; and is valuable for being the first production of the kind published in America, on a subject so painfully interesting." Despite the exaggeration contained in the last part of this statement, the poem possesses an undoubted interest, both as a characteristic example of Godfrey's verse in this manner and as a piece of descriptive poetry. The following lines from the poem have not infrequently been cited as a "striking picture of the deep distress that overwhelmed the frontier settlements in that epoch of unsparing savage warfare:"

Here no enchanting prospects yield delight,
But darksome forests intercept the sight;
Here fill'd with dread the trembling peasants go,
And start with terror at each nodding bough,
Nor as they trace the gloomy way along
Dare ask the influence of a chearing song.
  If in this wild a pleasing spot we meet,
In happier times some humble swain's retreat;
Where once with joy he saw the grateful soil
Yield a luxuriant harvest to his toil,

(Blest with content, enjoy'd his solitude,
And knew his pleasures, tho' of manners rude);
The lonely prospect strikes a secret dread,
While round the ravag'd Cott we silent tread,
Whose Owner fell beneath the savage hand,
Or roves a captive on some hostile land,
While the rich fields, with Ceres' blessings stor'd,
Grieve for their slaughter'd, or their absent lord.

The longer poems which Godfrey essayed, "The Court of Fancy", and "The Assembly of Birds" designated as "from Chaucer", both testify to his admiration for Chaucer as a poetic model. The latter poem begins at the thirteenth stanza of Chaucer's poem, "The Assembly of Fowls"; and the former poem is preceded by the outspoken confession of indebtedness to both Chaucer and Pope: "The learned reader need not be acquainted that the Author took the hint of the Transition from the Court of Fancy to that of Delusion, from Chaucer's Poem called the House of Fame, where the change is from the House of Fame to that of Rumour; and that he likewise had Mr. Pope's beautiful Poem on that subject in his eye, at the Time when he compos'd this Piece."

"The Court of Fancy" is filled with imaginative pictures, and reveals in rich measure the picturesque fancy of this youthful student of Chaucer and Pope. Perhaps none of his verse that has come down to us so conspicuously establishes his superiority to his American contemporaries of this pre-Revolutionary period — in poetic imagery, in lavish use of pictorial evocations, and in the pursuit of beauty for its own sake. Many of the descriptions, if no longer congenial to modern taste, certainly compare favorably with similar descriptions in the verse of Godfrey's models.

Take first this description of Fancy:—

High in the midst, rais'd on her rolling throne,
Sublimely eminent bright FANCY shone,
A glittering Tiara her temples bound,
Rich set with sparkling Rubies all around;
Her azure eyes roll'd with majestic grace,
And youth eternal bloom'd upon her face,
A radiant bough, Ensign of her command,
Of polish'd gold wav'd in her lilly hand;
The same the Sybil to *Æneas* gave,
When the bold *Trojan* cross'd the Stygian wave.
In silver traces fix'd unto her Car,
Four snowy Swans, proud of th' imperial Fair,
Wing'd lightly on, each in gay beauty drest,
Smooth'd the soft plumage that adorn'd her breast.
Sacred to her the lucent Chariot drew,
Or whether wildly thro' the air she flew,
Or whether to the dreary shades of Night
Oppress'd with gloom she downwards bent her flight,
Or proud aspiring sought the blest abodes,
And boldly shot among th' assembl'd Gods.

The transition is made from Fancy to Delusion, thus described:—

Now swiftly forward false Delusion came,
Wrapt in a fulvid Cloud appear'd the Dame.
Thin was her form, in airy garments drest,
And grotesque figures flam'd upon her vest;

JUVENILE POEMS

ON

VARIOUS SUBJECTS.

WITH THE

PRINCE OF PARTHIA,

A

T R A G E D Y.

BY THE LATE

Mr. *THOMAS GODFREY*, Junr.

of PHILADELPHIA.

To which is prefixed,

Some ACCOUNT of the *AUTHOR* and his *WRITINGS*.

Poeta nascitur non fit. HOR.

PHILADELPHIA,

Printed by HENRY MILLER, in Second-street,

MDCCLXV.

FACSIMILE OF TITLE-PAGE TO GODFREY'S COLLECTED POEMS

In her right hand she held a magic glass,
From whence around reflected glories pass.
Blind by the subtle rays, the giddy Croud
Rush'd wildly from the Dome and shouted loud.
The few remain'd whom Fancy did inspire
Yet undeceiv'd by vain Delusion's fire.

One notes not without amusement that in the ornate picture of the court, with the offspring of the Muses, Poetry, Painting, and Music, as attendants upon Fancy, Godfrey, like one of the Old Masters, has given himself a place no less modest than ridiculous:—

Close at her Feet a Bard in raptures lost,
Was plac'd, and wildly round his eye-balls tost;
Great Fancy was the theme! the soothing strain,
In floods of pleasure thrill'd thro' ev'ry vein.

It is a fundamental mistake to presume that Godfrey has only a most tenuous claim to critical attention, and that due entirely to the accidental fact of being the author of the first American tragedy. Aside from the question of fact involved in the claim made for "The Prince of Parthia", it cannot be denied that Godfrey's verse is at last beginning to be recognized as worthy of study. In his pleasing study of "Pennsylvania Poets of the Provincial Period",[1] Mr. Francis Howard Williams singles out for especial commendation the following lines from Godfrey's "Victory", which he characterizes as of "unusual brilliancy and color", with a haunting cadence strongly suggestive of the author of the "Elegy Written in a Country Churchyard":—

[1] *Pennsylvania Magazine of History and Biography;* April, 1893, p. 17.

One perfect Ruby was her glitt'ring throne,
  Gold were th' ascending steps, but smear'd with blood,
Close by her side bright laurel'd *Glory* shone,
  And *Fame* with her loud sounding Trumpet stood.

The entire production he speaks of as "a remarkable one, because it is so different from the prevailing manner of the time, and because it contains certain stanzas and single lines of real felicity." The graceful little poem, "The Wish", has a double interest for us — both because it seems undoubtedly to have inspired Oliver Wendell Holmes' "A Modest Wish", and also because in its opening lines Godfrey bespeaks the modest place which he seems destined to occupy: —

I only ask a mod'rate fate,
And tho' not in obscurity,
I would not yet be plac'd too high;
Between the two extreames I'd be,
Not meanly low, nor yet too great,
From both contempt and envy free.

In polite circles in Philadelphia, Godfrey was so much admired that after his death, the prime movers in collecting and publishing his literary remains included such men as Benjamin Franklin, who subscribed for the largest number of copies; Dr. William Smith, the Provost of the Academy; William Plumstead, in whose warehouse the Murray and Kean's Company opened their historic season in 1749; and Chief Justice William Allen who, fifteen years before, had officially expressed to the Common Council his fears that public performances of stage plays would be attended

THE

COURT OF FANCY;

A

POEM.

BY THOMAS GODFREY.

And as Imagination bodies forth
The Forms of Things unknown; the Poet's Pen
Turns them to Shape, and gives to airy Nothing
A local Habitation, and a Name.

SHAKESPEAR.

PHILADELPHIA:
Printed and Sold by WILLIAM DUNLAP, M,DCC,LXII.

FACSIMILE OF TITLE-PAGE "THE COURT OF FANCY"

with mischievous effects. Young Godfrey even achieved the distinction of being familiar author with society women of Philadelphia, satirically described by William Black as "female fishers for the reputation of wit"; in 1773, Miss Sarah Eve records in her journal that she is reminded of "those lines of our poet Godfrey: [1]

'Curiosity's another name for man,
The blazing meteor streaming thro' the air
Commands our wonder, and admiring eyes,
With eager gaze we trace the lucent path,
'Til spent at length it shrinks to native nothing.
While the bright stars which ever steady glow,
Unheeded shine, and bless the world below.'"

Godfrey's severest and most meticulous critic was his friend and patron, Provost Smith, who recognized in him a genius undeveloped. His final verdict upon the poems, therefore, has for us a peculiar interest — a verdict which concludes the "Postscript" he prepared for the collected edition of Godfrey's poems: —

"Upon the whole, I persuade myself that, the severest critic, looking over smaller matters, will allow these writings of Mr. Godfrey, to be aptly characteriz'd, in the following lines from the Court of Fancy —

'Bold Fancy's hand th' amazing pile uprears,
In every part stupendous skill appears;
In beautiful disorder, yet compleat,
The structure shines irregularly great.'"

[1] "The Prince of Parthia." Closing lines of Scene II, Act I.

IX.

The first historian of the American theatre, in speaking of "The Prince of Parthia", categorically states: "Whether intended for the stage, or only for the closet, is unknown. That it was not performed by the players is certain." [1] This statement is inaccurate in two particulars. In the first place, we have already seen that the play was intended for the stage; and in the second, there is no reason to doubt that it was performed. The *Pennsylvania Journal* of April 23, 1767, published an announcement that "The Prince of Parthia, a Tragedy, written in America, by the late ingenious, Mr. Godfrey, of this City, will be presented to-morrow at the New Theatre, in Southwark, by the American Company." [2] This announcement contained a list of the principal actors in the company; but unfortunately there has been discovered no account or criticism of the *première* of the first American tragedy.[3] Seilhamer, the historian of the early American stage, has suggested a cast which, because of his minute study of the plays and

[1] "A History of the American Theatre", by William Dunlap (N. Y. 1832), p. 27.

[2] A similar, though briefer, announcement appeared on the same date in the *Pennsylvania Gazette.*

[3] There is no reason to doubt that the play was produced as announced; and there has been found no announcement of its withdrawal in any subsequent advertisement of the American Company. A week before Godfrey's play was announced, players, who were headed by the younger Hallam at that time, advertised the coming performance of *The Disappointment,* an anonymous comic opera, or farce, by Colonel Thomas Forrest. This comic piece was recognized as being too broad for public representation, and the company made announcement that it had been withdrawn. Had Godfrey's play been withdrawn, doubtless a similar advertisement would have followed.

players of the period, may be accepted as very probable, with the possible exception of the minor rôles. The suggested cast is as follows:—

Artabanus, King of Parthia	Mr. Douglass
Arsaces (his Sons)	Mr. Hallam
Vardanes (his Sons)	Mr. Tomlinson
Gotarzes (his Sons)	Mr. Wall
Barzaphernes, Lieutenant-General, under Arsaces	Mr. Allyn
Lysias (Officers at Court)	Mr. Broadbelt
Phraates (Officers at Court)	Mr. Greville
Bethas, a Noble Captive	Mr. Morris
Thermusa, the Queen	Mrs. Douglass
Evanthe, belov'd by Arsaces	Miss Cheer
Cleone, her confident	Miss Wainwright
Edessa, Attendant on the Queen	Mrs. Morris.[1]

The author of "A Colonial Officer and his Times" hazards the surmise that "The Prince of Parthia", doubtless during the sessions of the North Carolina Legislature, "was put on the boards by the amateurs of Wilmington and greeted with thunders of applause." No evidence in support of this surmise has yet been brought forward. It may not come amiss to observe that professional actors of distinction played in North Carolina in this early period. In a letter to the Bishop of London, June 11, 1768, written from Brunswick, North Carolina, Governor William Tryon recommends for ordination orders a talented young actor named Giffard, who gave as his reason for desiring to enter the ministry "that he was most wearied of the

[1] "History of the American Theatre", I, 194.

vague life of his present profession, and fully persuaded he could employ his talents to more benefit to society by going into holy orders and superintending the education of youth in this Province." Clearly the type of dramatic performance given in North Carolina by Giffard and his company was of a high order; for Governor Tryon, a gentleman of cosmopolitan culture, thus concludes his letter: "If your Lordship grants Mr. Giffard his petition, you will take off the best player on the American Stage." [1]

Upon more than one occasion, it has been stated that "The Prince of Parthia" was once produced in Wilmington, North Carolina.[2] After extended and laborious researches, especially in the newspapers of Wilmington and of Raleigh, I finally discovered the following paragraph, in an editorial under the caption "The Prince of Parthia", in the *News and Observer* of Raleigh, N. C., February 6, 1890: [3]

"We have an impression that the piece used to be in vogue among amateur actors before the war (*i.e.*,

[1] *N. C. Colonial Records*, VII, 786–7.

[2] "Libraries and Literature in North Carolina in the Eighteenth Century" (1896), in which the author, Dr. S. B. Weeks, states (p. 244) that "The Prince of Parthia" was presented by amateurs "at the old theatre there (Wilmington) about 1847"; "Wilmington" in "Historic Towns of the Southern States", edited by L. P. Powell, 1904, in which Bishop J. B. Cheshire states (p. 244) that "The Prince of Parthia" was written in Wilmington in 1759, and "was years afterwards produced on the stage by a company of local amateurs." Upon appeal to these gentlemen for information, neither was able to cite me to the authority for the above-quoted statements.

[3] The editor at this date was Captain Samuel A. Ashe, a native of Wilmington, and the historian of North Carolina.

Lewis Hallam
Who played the title-rôle in The Prince of Parthia, Southwark Theater, April 24, 1767

the War between the States). Indeed we think that it and 'Box and Cox' were the first pieces we ever saw. It was a performance by the Thespians at the Old Theatre at Wilmington about 1847." [1]

During the first half of the nineteenth century, a remarkable amateur dramatic organization flourished at Wilmington, North Carolina. At the time he held command of all the colonial forces in Virginia during the French and Indian war, Colonel James Innes endowed the famous Academy there which afterwards bore his name.[2] This was the first private bequest for educational purposes in the history of North Carolina. Although the Academy was incorporated in 1783, the building was not erected until about the year 1800, when the number of inhabitants of Wilmington was scarcely more than fifteen hundred. "Before the completion of the Academy building", says the antiquarian, Col. James Green Burr, "a theatrical corps had been organized in Wilmington, and an arrangement was made between them and the Trustees of the Academy that the lower part of the building should be fitted up and used exclusively as a Theatre, which arrangement was carried out by a perpetual lease which was made to the Thalian Association, the then and last name of the only the-

[1] In all probability this was the authority for the statements cited in a footnote (2), p. 52.

[2] Col. Innes, who may well have formed the acquaintance of Thomas Godfrey, resided at his seat, "Point Pleasant", about seven miles from Wilmington. He died at Wilmington on September 25, 1759. His will, endowing "a free school for the benefit of the youth of North Carolina", was made at Winchester, Va., on July 4, 1754, and probated at Newbern, Oct. 9, 1759.

atrical organization that ever existed in Wilmington."[1] The Association passed through various stages of decline and revival, during the first half of the nineteenth century; its fourth and last revival occurred in 1847. It is certainly probable that, in testimony of their pride in the circumstance that the first American tragedy was written in Wilmington and by a poet of brilliant promise, the Thalian Association produced "The Prince of Parthia." A careful examination of the files of the *Wilmington Journal* for the years 1847 and 1848 reveals no explicit notice of the performance of this play; but the evidence of Captain Ashe, who doubtless referred to "the Thalians" when he described the company as "the Thespians" (a generic term also for theatrical performers), is reenforced by the circumstance that the farce, "Box and Cox", recalled by him in conjunction with "The Prince of Parthia", was produced by the Thalian Association[2] — on July 7, 1848, and probably a number of times before that date and after April 30, 1847, when the Association was reorganized. The performance of "The Prince of Parthia" from the evidence before us, most probably occurred, if at all, on June 11, 1847, when the performance of a play not mentioned by title, is highly praised in the *Journal*.[3]

[1] "The Thalian Association of Wilmington, N. C., with Sketches of Many of its Members. By a Member of the Association." Wilmington, N. C. 1871. For the use of a copy of this very rare pamphlet, I am indebted to the kindness of Mr. Clayton Giles of Wilmington.

[2] *Wilmington Journal.*

[3] In testimony of the elaborate repertory of the Thalian Association, the following partial list of plays produced by this remarkable dramatic company during the years 1847 and 1848 may prove of interest: "The Lady of

When the superb historical pageant was staged in Philadelphia on October 9, 1908, one of the most striking scenes presented was the impressive opening scene from the first act of Godfrey's tragedy, which depicts the return of the victorious Prince of Parthia. This scene was arranged by Mr. Joseph Jackson, an authority on the history of Philadelphia; the costumes were designed by the well-known artist, Mr. Guernsey Moore, of Swarthmore; and the characters were impersonated by the members of the Enterprise Dramatic Club, of Germantown, the birthplace of Thomas Godfrey, the elder.[1]

Acting under the belief that Thomas Godfrey was a member of the Academy which, with the College of Philadelphia, formed the nucleus of the University of Pennsylvania, the Zelosophic Society of that institution gave a performance of "The Prince of Parthia" in the New Century Drawing Room, on Friday, March 26, 1915 — almost a century and a half after the first performance of the play. The likelihood of a performance having taken place at Wilmington, N. C. in 1747 has not been hitherto known to students of the American drama; and the program of the per-

Lyons", and "'Tis All a Farce" ("the first performance of the season", Nov. 26, 1847), "Lend Me Five Shillings," "Speed the Plough", "Hunting the Turtle", "Feudal Times, or The Court of James the Third", "The Irish Attorney or Galway Practice in 1770", "The Poor Gentleman", "The Omnibus", "The Honey Moon", "State Secrets", "The Jew and the Doctor", "The Invisible Prince of the Island of Tranquil Delight", "The Gamester", "The Point of Honor", "London Assurance", "Damon and Pythias."

[1] *Cf.* "The Book of the Pageant", by J. Jackson, and arranged by E. P. Oberholtzer. Philadelphia, 1908, p. 20. For data concerning the pageant, I am indebted to Messrs. Oberholtzer, Moore, and Jackson.

formance by the Zelosophic Society contained the statement: "The production of 'The Prince of Parthia' by the Zelosophic Society marks the first representation of the play since April 24, 1767." The play was produced by this ancient dramatic society of the University of Pennsylvania, which was organized as early as 1829, at the suggestion of Professor A. H. Quinn, the first secretary of the society upon its reorganization in 1892. Godfrey's tragedy was given, without scenery, under the direction of Mrs. Sara F. T. Price; and the exquisite costumes, which represented elaborate historical research, were designed by Mr. and Mrs. Guernsey Moore, of Swarthmore. "Although the play has little action and shows the earmarks of an inexperienced dramatist", one reads in the account of the performance in *The Pennsylvanian* of March 27, 1915, "the attention of the audience was sustained from beginning to end by the sincerity and concentration of the cast." The performance was preceded by a brief address by Professor Quinn, tracing Godfrey's life in part, and in especial touching upon his connection with the University of Pennsylvania, as a student of the Academy.[1] "The Society feels very gratified over the results of its production," writes Mr. Francis J. Carr, Chairman Zelosophic Society Dramatic Committee for the production of "The Prince of Parthia." "We were a little uncertain as to whether the play would take well, but thought it worth while to try. Previously we had always given a modern comedy, but decided this year to try historic American drama, and so chose 'The Prince of Parthia.'

[1] *Cf.* letter of A. H. Quinn, *The Nation*, April 15, 1915.

Triumphal Return of the Prince of Parthia
Philadelphia Pageant, October 9, 1908

The interest shown was even above our expectations, and we consider that the play was the biggest success of any that we have given. The comments on the play were very generally favorable. Dean Quinn, of the College, who attended the play, said he was surprised to see how the lines seemed to hold the attention of the audience, even though the action was rather slow and perhaps imperfect. The fact of the excellence of the lines themselves, as written by Godfrey, was something that impressed us particularly in working up the play."

X.

It is customary for Godfrey's biographers, with the inaccuracy of ignorance, to state that his play is based upon an ancient story. As a matter of fact, one of the most significant features of the play is that, whereas it deals with certain historical figures, in arbitrary relations, drawn from the story of the kingdom of Parthia, the drama itself — the plot — is wholly the heir of Godfrey's invention. A brief survey of the historical characters and episodes utilized will serve to exhibit Godfrey's real originality, and his skill in constructing an effective plot from the most sterile material.

That section of country, some three hundred and twenty miles east and west, and nearly two hundred miles north and south, east of the Caspian Sea and in the region lying south of the present Khorassan, was the domain of the Parthian kingdom. Its history belongs to the history of Persia, Greece, and Rome. It is important to observe that, just as the king of the Roman Empire was denominated Cæsar, so the ruler of the Parthian kingdom was termed Arsaces.

In Godfrey's play, the characters who play the leading rôles and are interlinked in the action, are Thermusa, Vonones, Artabanus, Vardanes, and Gotarzes. As stated by Godfrey in the Preface to the play, Thermusa was "not the wife of King Artabanus, but (according to Tacitus, Strabo, and Josephus) of Phraates; Artabanus being the fourth King of Parthia after him."[1] In fact, Musa, an Italian slave-girl, was the wife of Phraates IV, the parricide, who reigned from 37 B.C. to 2 B.C.; and her son, Phraataces, conspired with her to slay his own father, and seizing the throne, made her at once queen and concubine.[2] He paid her the extravagant tribute of violating all historical tradition and placing her effigy upon his coins. The name, Thermusa, as used by Godfrey, is an error — due to the fact that the coins bore the fulsome flatteries paid her by Phraataces, the inscriptions reading not merely "Queen", but "Heavenly Goddess." Authentic specimens of Parthian coins bear the inscription, ΜΟΥϹΗϹ ΒΑϹΙΛΙϹϹΗϹ ΘΕΑϹ ΟΥΡΑΝΙΑϹ. So that the θερμοῦσα of Josephus, whence Godfrey clearly derived the name, was an evident blunder, due to himself or to his scribe, for θεὰ Μοῦσα. The Parthian queen not only assumed the title θεὰ, but also identified herself with the Muse Urania.[3]

[1] *Cf.* Josephus, *Ant. Jud.*, xviii, 2, § 4; Tacitus, *Ann.*, II, xi and xii; Strabo, xi, 9, § 2 and xv, i, § 36.

[2] Josephus, *Ant. Jud.*, xviii, 2, § 4.

[3] "Catalogue of the Coins of Parthia." By Warrick Wroth. London, 1903, Introduction, pp. xl and xli.

Vonones, eldest son of Phraates IV and Musa, was elevated to the throne of Parthia, after the assassination of Orodes in A.D. 8; but proving weak and effeminate, he was displaced by Artabanus III after a reign of only two years. In 34, Artabanus seized the Armenian throne, and appointed his eldest son, who bore the name as well as the title of Arsaces, to be king. In 35 A.D. Arsaces was murdered by his attendants at the instigation of Pharasmanes, King of Iberia, who usurped the Armenian throne.

Following the death of Artabanus III, probably in A.D. 40, his two sons, Vardanes and Gotarzes, became rival claimants to the throne. The choice fell upon Gotarzes; but soon the nobles, revolted by his brutality in murdering his brother, Artabanus, together with his wife and son, deposed him, and placed Vardanes on the throne. After a succession of struggles between the two brothers, Vardanes in A.D. 45 fell a victim to a conspiracy, being murdered while hunting; and Gotarzes, now sole ruler, occupied the throne until his death in A.D. 51.[1]

Thus it will be seen that in this welter of parricide, fratricide, assassination, and incest, there is no motived dramatic story ready to the hand of Godfrey. From these barren materials he draws only the names, not the precise characters, of the historic personages; and utilizes only the relentless ambition of the brothers, Vardanes and Gotarzes, for their father's throne, hav-

[1] *Cf.* "The Sixth Great Oriental Monarchy", by G. Rawlinson, N. Y., pp. 215–251. "Mémoire sur la chronologie et l'iconographie des Rois Parthes Arsacides", by A. de Longperier, Paris, 1853–1882. "A View of the History and Coinage of the Parthians", by J. Lindsay, Cork, 1852.

ing as one result the murder by Gotarzes of his second brother, Artabanus, whom Godfrey identifies with Arsaces.[1]

XI.

During recent years, research has brought to light scattered records of productions and publications of plays in America far earlier than was imagined by William Dunlap, the first historian of the American theatre. If we do not confine our attention to the present bounds of the United States, we find that the first play both written and acted in North America was the masque, "Le Théâtre de Neptune en la Nouvelle-France", by Marc Lescarbot. This play was performed at Port-Royal, Acadie, on November 14, 1606, in honor of the return of Lescarbot's chief, the Sieur de Poutrincourt, from the country of the Armouchiquois.[2] In 1640, Father Le Jeune and the Jesuit missionaries added certain American scenes to a French tragi-comedy, the title of which is unknown, and produced it at Quebec at some time shortly prior to September 10, 1640, in honor of Monseigneur the Dauphin.[3] The earliest record of a performance of a play within the present bounds of the United States sets forth that in 1655 a play, known as "Ye Beare and Ye Club", was acted in Accomac County on the eastern shore of Virginia by three citizens, Cornelius

[1] For assistance in the historical investigation I am indebted to Mr. Herbert Putnam, of the Library of Congress, and to Mr. Joseph Jastrow, Jr., of the Library of the University of Pennsylvania.

[2] This masque is contained in a volume, "Les Muses de la Nouvelle-France", Paris, 1609. *Cf.* F. L. Gay: *Nation*, Feb. 11, 1909.

[3] Account of Paul Le Jeune in the "Jesuit Relations", dated Kébec, September 10, 1640. *Cf.* W. J. Neidig: *Nation*, Jan. 28, 1909.

Persons of the Play

Designs by Guernsey Moore

Wilkinson, Philip Howard, and William Darby.[1] The rare volume by Anthony Aston, published about 1730, shows that there was play-acting in Charleston, South Carolina, and in New York at some time prior to 1702. In speaking of his arrival in this country, Aston, who had been an actor in the West Indies, says: "I arrived, after many vicissitudes, at Charles-Town full of shame, poverty, nakedness and hunger; turned play-actor and poet, and wrote a play of one act on the country." Whether the play was ever published or produced is not known.

The first play written and published by a resident of what is now the United States, so far as is at present known, was "Androboros", by Robert Hunter, Colonial Governor of New York, issued in 1714.[2] It was not until 1751, it appears, that another play was published in this country, namely "The Suspected Daughter; or, Jealous Father", a "farce in three acts, both serious and comic", by T. T. This play, which was printed in Boston, is probably the first play written by a native American to be published within the present bounds of the United States.

"The Prince of Parthia", published in 1765, still holds unchallenged the claim made for it, of being not only the first tragedy written by an American, and published in America, but also the first play written by an American to be performed upon the professional stage. "The Père Indien", by Le Blanc Villeneuve, and written while he was in the French

[1] *Cf.* Philip Alexander Bruce: *Nation,* Feb. 11, 1909.

[2] "Early American Plays. 1714–1830." By Oscar Wegelin. 2d edition, revised. N. Y. 1905.

service in Louisiana, was produced in 1753 in the Governor's mansion in New Orleans — but there is no reason to believe that this play was performed by a professional company; and it is uncertain whether his play, "Poucha-Houmma", based upon a story he had heard while employed by the government among the Tchactas (1752–1758), was either published or produced.[1] The first American comedy, or comic opera, as it was called, that was accepted by a manager and put into rehearsal for production, was "The Disappointment; or The Farce of Credulity", by Colonel Thomas Forrest, of Germantown, under the pseudonym of "Andrew Barton, Esq." It was announced for production on April 20 by Mr. Douglass' company, at the Southwark Theatre, in Goddard's *Pennsylvania Chronicle* of April 18, 1767. It was announced as "just published" in the same issue of the paper. Doubtless because of its coarseness and immoral tone, it was hurriedly withdrawn; although a different reason was assigned in the announcement in the *Pennsylvania Gazette* on the following Wednesday: "'The Disappointment' (that was advertised for Monday), as it contains personal reflections, is unfit for the stage." The conjunction of the first American comedy accepted for professional production with the first American tragedy, written, accepted, and produced, is remarkable. For it is scarcely open to question that "The Prince of Parthia", by a native Philadelphian, was produced to banish the popular disappointment incident to the withdrawal of "The Disappointment" by Colonel Forrest, whose local repute

[1] Alcée Fortier: Modern Language Association, 1886.

as a wag had raised high expectations of amusement. The tragedy followed immediately upon the withdrawal of the comedy, as evidenced by the announcement in the *Pennsylvania Gazette* of April 23, 1767.[1]

XII.

Among the influences which left their impress upon Godfrey and find betrayal in "The Prince of Parthia", we must reckon the "Cato" of Addison. And this as acted drama, no less than as a work of literature; for it is probable that Godfrey saw this play produced in Philadelphia. The richness of the Eastern background and the barbaric features of the setting may well have been influential factors with Godfrey in his choice of situation and *locale.* Certainly, the deficiency of animated action in Addison's play is paralleled in Godfrey's tragedy. Nevertheless, we readily observe that the poetic fervor and youthful spirit of Godfrey accord more nearly with the challenging tone of Marlowe, his comic bombast and "high-resounding terms", than they reflect the cold sententiousness and elegant, if lifeless, "correctness" of Addison. "Tamburlaine the Great", both in atmosphere and setting, was perhaps a more suggestive source for Godfrey than "Cato" — even although he never had the former produced before him on the stage. Other minor influences may well have been operative; for as long as two years before its publication, "The Prince of Parthia" was known to a small circle of library *illuminati* in Philadelphia and described in the

[1] G. O. Seilhamer: "History of the American Theatre before the Revolution", 1888, I, chapters XVII and XVIII.

Pennsylvania Gazette, perhaps by George Webbe or Samuel Keimer, Godfrey's fellow-craftsmen, in 1763, at the time of Godfrey's death, as a tragedy which "breathes all the Pathos of Otway."

Godfrey's most unquestioned inspiration, however, — from the opening scene descriptive of Arsaces' triumphal return to the final scene of the suicide of Arsaces and Evanthe — is none other than the author of "Hamlet", "Macbeth", "Romeo and Juliet", "Julius Cæsar", and "As You Like It." One of the most striking parallels is the resemblance of the scene in Godfrey's play, in which the Ghost appears (Act IV, Scene 5), to the corresponding scene in "Hamlet", Act III, Scene 4. Hamlet's visit to the Queen is made with the intention of upbraiding her sorely; and the apparition of the ghost of Hamlet's father strengthens him in the execution of his intention. With due attention to the difference in the situations, Thermusa visits her son Arsaces but is so struck with terror by the apparition as to be deterred from her murderous purpose. The similarity is carried further still, since the Ghost in Godfrey's play is apparent only to Thermusa just as in Shakespeare's play the Ghost is an hallucination perceived by Hamlet alone. Compare the lines in this passage from "The Prince of Parthia":—

Ghost of Artabanus rises.

QUEEN.

Save me — oh! — save me — ye eternal pow'rs —
See! — See it comes, surrounded with dread terrors —
Hence — hence! nor blast me with that horrid sight —

. . . .

PERSONS OF THE PLAY
Designs by Guernsey Moore

ARSACES.

Your eyes seem fix'd upon some dreadful object,
Horror and anguish cloath your whiten'd face.
And your frame shakes with terror; I hear you speak
As seeming earnest in discourse, yet hear
No second voice.

QUEEN.

What! saw'st thou nothing?

ARSACES.

Nothing.

QUEEN.

Nor hear'd? —

ARSACES.

Nor hear'd.

with the following lines from "Hamlet": —

Enter GHOST.

HAMLET.

Save me, and hover o'er me with your wings,
You heavenly guards! . . . .

QUEEN.

Alas, how is't with you,
That you do bend your eye on vacancy,
And with the incorporal air do hold discourse?
Forth at your eyes your spirits wildly peep;
. . . .
. . . . Whereon do you look?

HAMLET.

On him, on him! Look you, how pale he glares!
. . . . Do not look upon me;

Lest, with this piteous action you convert
My stern effects: then what I have to do
Will want true colour! tears perchance for blood.

QUEEN.

To whom do you speak this?

HAMLET.

Do you see nothing there?

QUEEN.

Nothing at all; yet all that is I see.

HAMLET.

Nor did you nothing hear?

QUEEN.

No, nothing but ourselves.

And again we set Gertrude's "Alas! he's mad!" beside the exclamation of Arsaces: "Alas, her sense is lost . . .!" The Ghost in Godfrey's play, like Banquo's ghost in "Macbeth" is not a character in the play, but merely a figment of Thermusa's disordered fancy; and Godfrey is bold enough in his plagiarism to insert Macbeth's remark to the ghost (III, iv, 49–50):—

"Never shake
Thy gory locks at me."

in the mouth of Thermusa:—

Ah! frown not on me —
Why dost you shake thy horrid locks at me?

Equally striking is the resemblance between the description by Gotarzes of the rescue of Vardanes from the Euphrates by Arsaces (I, i, 96–106) with the description from Shakespeare's "Julius Cæsar" (I, 2, 99–114), by Cassius in the first person of his rescue of Cæsar from the Tiber.[1] The parallel, with its theme of ingratitude in both, stands out on comparison of the two passages printed below:—

GOTARZES.

'Twas summer last, as we
Were bathing in *Euphrates'* flood, *Vardanes*
Proud of strength would seek the further shore;
But 'ere he the mid-stream gain'd, a poignant pain
Shot thro' his well-strung nerves, contracting all,
And the stiff joints refus'd their wonted aid.
Loudly he cried for help, *Arsaces* heard,
And thro' the swelling waves he rush'd to save
His drowning Brother, and gave him life,
And for the boon the Ingrate pays him hate.

CASSIUS.

For once, upon a raw and gusty day
The troubled Tiber chafing with her shores,
Cæsar said to me, "Darest thou, Cassius, now
Leap in with me into this angry flood,
And swim to yonder point?" Upon the word,
Accoutred as I was, I plunged in,

[1] This parallel was called to my attention by Professor C. Alphonso Smith.

And bade him follow: so indeed he did.
The torrent roared, and we did buffet it
With lusty sinews, throwing it aside
And stemming it with hearts of controversy;
But ere we could arrive the point proposed,
Cæsar cried, "Help me, Cassius, or I sink."
I, as Æneas our great ancestor
Did from the flames of Troy upon his shoulder
The old Anchises bear, so from the waves of Tiber
Did I the tired Cæsar: and this man
Is now become a god, and Cassius is
A wretched creature, and must bend his body
If Cæsar but carelessly nod on him.

There is a resemblance, though less obvious, between Orlando's rescue of his brother from the lioness in "As You Like It" (IV, iii, 98–132) and Arsaces' rescue of Gotarzes from the leopard (I, i, 57–75). An equally striking utilization of a famous Shakespearean episode and its handling is revealed in the final scene of "The Prince of Parthia", "Romeo and Juliet" affording the model. We see Evanthe, under the mistaken notion that Arsaces is dead, take poison; and when Arsaces discovers the tragic fact and holds the dead Evanthe in his arms, he, like Romeo, takes his own life. Perhaps one should not quarrel with Vardanes for the employment of Shakespearean phrases such as

> "This many-headed monster multitude,
> Unsteady is as giddy fortune's wheel
> As woman fickle, varying as the wind;"

which is a combination of the expression "many-headed multitude" from "Coriolanus" (II, iii, 16–17) and the line from "Henry V" (III, vi, 28):

"And giddy fortune's furious fickle wheel."

In spite of these bold plagiarisms and appropriations, more or less justified, from Shakespeare — all of which should not be merely imputed as faults in the twenty-three year old Godfrey, but possess peculiar interest as testifying to his diligent study of the greatest of all models, — "The Prince of Parthia" is a work of very considerable individual merits. It seems to me to be a merit, rather than a demerit, that Godfrey in this drama does not strictly observe the "unities" of the classic formula, which was on his part an independent deviation from the custom. Williams praises the play for its "passages of great nobility", and rightly regards it as "an essential element in the literary product of the (Provincial) period." In particular, he notes: "The love-story is delicate and tender, and Godfrey, in his arrangement of the sequence of his scenes, has displayed a sense of law of contrast, — a quality in which the Colonial poets were strangely deficient." [1] This play contains enough original thought, for all its manifest derivations, and enough poetic sensibility, for all its oblique reflections, to give it strength, beauty, and individual character. In reading the play we must also remember, in extenuation of some of its defects, such as elisions, unfinished lines, and misplaced accents, that it was left in an unfinished state, especially the last act, owing to Godfrey's haste in transmitting the original manuscript

[1] *Pennsylvania Magazine of History and Biography*, April, 1893.

to Philadelphia, in the hope of having it produced upon the stage there. One may quote with approval the sensible observation of Nathaniel Evans: —

"He (Evans) would only beg leave, therefore, to remark of the Tragedy the *Prince of Parthia* — That it is the first essay which our Province, or perhaps this Continent, has, as yet, exhibited of Dramatic Composition — and, that there is possibly some merit even in endeavouring to overcome noble difficulties, though we should happen to aspire after a flight beyond our years.

'In great attempts 'tis glorious e'en to fall.'"

XIII.

A diligent research which I have made in regard to the last resting-place of the remains of Thomas Godfrey has finally led to the identification of the spot. In 1747 or 1748 Michael Higgins, one of the original settlers of Wilmington, a faithful and well tried friend of the Church, presented to the Parish of St. James in Wilmington a lot on the corner of present Market and Fourth streets. This lot not being sufficiently large for the double purpose of a church edifice and a burying ground, the Legislature of the province passed an act by which the vestry was authorized to use thirty feet of Market street for the front of the street; and this accounts for the location of the old building partly in the street.[1] Nineteen years elapsed from the commencement to the completion of the first parish church

[1] This act, which is the first found on record touching the parish, is in Martin's collection of private laws of the State, and bears date XXV Geo. II., 1751. The old building was removed in 1839.

Where Thomas Godfrey Lies
Old St. James' Churchyard, Wilmington, North Carolina

of St. James. The commissioners named for carrying into effect the provisions of the original act of 1751 were Samuel Swann, Joseph Blake, William Faris, John Sampson, Lewis De Rosset and John Ashe, members of his Majesty's Council. From the preamble of this act it appears that the church was expected to be built by the voluntary contributions of parishioners. By another act, bearing date XI Geo. III., 1770, ch. xiii, also found in Martin, the Hon. Lewis De Rosset and Frederick Gregg, Esq., are appointed commissioners in the place of John Dubois and George Wakely, deceased, for finishing the church in Wilmington.[1] It was while the old St. James' Church was in course of construction, namely on August 3, 1763, that Thomas Godfrey died in Wilmington; and his remains were laid to rest in St. James' Churchyard. His grave was marked with a monument of some description, which was undoubtedly still standing as late as 1846, for in "An Imperfect Sketch of the History of the Town of Wilmington", written by the brilliant biographer of James Iredell, Griffith J. McRee, it is categorically stated in regard to Thomas Godfrey: "His grave is designated by a tombstone in the burial ground attached to St. James' Church." [2] There can

[1] "Sketch of St. James's Parish", Wilmington, N. C., by "a member of the vestry", N. Y., 1874, pp. 15–17. The author of this pamphlet was the distinguished antiquarian, the late Colonel James Green Burr. This pamphlet is an elaboration of the "Historical Notices of St. James's Parish, Wilmington", 1843, by the Rev. Robert B. Drane, D. D., sometime rector of the parish.

[2] For this information I am indebted to Mr. William B. McKoy, the historian of Wilmington, who has supplied me with copies of the original article by McRee, in two parts, which appeared in the *Wilmington Chronicle*, Sept. 2 and 16, 1846.

be no doubt on this score; for it is supplemented by the statement of John Fanning Watson, who, in his *Annals of Philadelphia*, observes in regard to Thomas Godfrey: "His remains were designated there (Wilmington, North Carolina) by a tombstone, in the ground of St. James' Church.[1] Many of the old headstones and footstones to the graves have long since crumbled into dust; a number are piled up near the present church. A most careful search, which I made in the summer of 1915, failed to bring to light Godfrey's tombstone. As long ago as some years prior to 1890, it is certain that Godfrey's tombstone had disappeared; for in an address in the Opera House in Wilmington, on February 3, 1890, entitled "The Old Churchyard of St. James", the historian and antiquarian, Col. James Green Burr, lifts aside for a brief moment the veil which hides from our curious gaze the young poet and his brief span of life on the lower Cape Fear: —

"Some years ago, in the Spring time of the year it was, and long before the present so-called improvements had been made upon the grounds, I strolled into the old burial place of the dead. . . . It is now almost deserted and greatly changed, but at the time of my visit, tall trees waved their untrimmed branches over the graves of those who once trod our streets, the rank undergrowth grew over many an old sandstone slab, bearing a brief notice of the last resting place and virtues of the departed. It was towards the close of day, and the mild beams of the sun shone with tempered radiance. Here — there, all around me the

[1] Vol. I, p. 531, 1877 edition.

graves of those who in former years carried life and it may be happiness within the social circle. . . . Thomas Godfrey, the son of the inventor of the quadrant, and the author of the first dramatic work written in America, lies buried in that old church yard. His grave is undistinguished from those of the numerous congregation of the dead sleeping around him. Time has long since levelled the incumbent sod, and no stones were erected to mark the spot where his ashes repose. The memorials of him are few." [1]

In this famous old churchyard there sleep in death Thomas Godfrey's erstwhile friend, once clamant voice of revolution, Cornelius Harnett, upon whose headstone, still standing, are engraved the lines from Pope's "Essay on Man":—

"Slave to no sect, he took no private road,
But looked through Nature up to Nature's God;" [2]

and the parents of Captain Johnston Blakeley, the famous naval hero of the War of 1812, about whose mysterious loss at sea while in the flush of young manhood romance still weaves its legends. A clue to the location of Godfrey's grave is afforded in the statement made by Griffith J. McRee, who had seen the tombstone, that Godfrey's remains "lie in St. James' Churchyard, not very far from the grave of Harnett." [3] The exact spot was very closely located in my presence

[1] *James Sprunt Historical Monograph,* No. 4. University of North Carolina, Chapel Hill, N. C., 1904, pp. 125–126. Colonel Burr was unaware of the fact that there had been a tombstone over Godfrey's grave, which was standing as late as 1846, a fact specifically stated by McRee.

[2] Epistle IV, lines 31–2.

[3] "Life and Correspondence of James Iredell", New York, 1858, II, appendix, p. 601.

by Mr. Eugene Martin, antiquarian authority of Wilmington — the spot being some forty odd feet from Harnett's grave, in a line directed toward the middle of the church.

In his "Elegy to the Memory of Thomas Godfrey", dated October 1, 1763, his devoted friend, Nathaniel Evans, thus begins the last stanza: —

"Stranger, who e'er thou art, by fortune's hand
Tost on the baleful *Carolinian* strand,
Oh! if thou seest perchance the Poet's grave
The sacred spot with tears of sorrow lave;
Oh! shade it, shade it with ne'er fading bays.
Hallowed the place where gentle GODFREY lays." [1]

May the time be not far distant when the pious wish of Evans shall be realized, and a fitting and permanent memorial be erected over the grave of Thomas Godfrey, concerning whom and whose work the distinguished historian of American literature, Professor Moses Coit Tyler, has said: "Thomas Godfrey is a true poet, and 'The Prince of Parthia' is a noble beginning of dramatic literature in America."

ARCHIBALD HENDERSON.

[1] This Elegy was published in the *Gentleman's Magazine*, of London, December, 1764.

THE PRINCE OF PARTHIA

A TRAGEDY

Parthian Coins

1. Musa
2. Vonones I
3. Artabanus III
4. Gotarzes
5. Vardanes I

Dramatis Personæ

Men

Artabanus, King of Parthia.
Arsaces, } his Sons.
Vardanes, } his Sons.
Gotarzes, } his Sons.
Barzaphernes, Lieutenant-General, under Arsaces.
Lysias, } Officers at Court.
Phraates, } Officers at Court.
Bethas, a Noble Captive.

Women

Thermusa, the Queen.
Evanthe, belov'd by Arsaces.
Cleone, her Confident.
Edessa, Attendant on the Queen.

Guards and Attendants

Scene, CTESIPHON

ADVERTISEMENT

Our Author has made Use of the *licentia poetica* in the Management of this Dramatic Piece; and deviates, in a particular or two, from what is agreed on by Historians: The Queen *Thermusa* being not the Wife of King *Artabanus*, but (according to *Tacitus*, *Strabo* and *Josephus*) of *Phraates; Artabanus* being the fourth King of *Parthia* after him. Such Lapses are not unprecedented among the Poets; and will the more readily admit of an Excuse, when the Voice of History is followed in the Description of Characters.

The PRINCE of PARTHIA

A TRAGEDY

ACT I. SCENE I.

The Temple of the Sun.

GOTARZES AND PHRAATES.

GOTARZES.

He comes, *Arsaces* comes, my gallant Brother
(Like shining Mars in all the pomp of conquest)
Triumphant enters now our joyful gates;
Bright Victory waits on his glitt'ring car,
And shows her fav'rite to the wond'ring croud;
While Fame exulting sounds the happy name
To realms remote, and bids the world admire.
Oh! 'tis a glorious day: — let none presume
T' indulge the tear, or wear the gloom of sorrow;
This day shall shine in Ages yet to come,
And grace the Parthian story.

PHRAATES.

Glad *Ctes'phon*
Pours forth her numbers, like a rolling deluge,
To meet the blooming Hero; all the ways,

On either side, as far as sight can stretch,
Are lin'd with crouds, and on the lofty walls
Innumerable multitudes are rang'd.
On ev'ry countenance impatience sate
With roving eye, before the train appear'd.
But when they saw the Darling of the Fates,
They rent the air with loud repeated shouts;
The Mother show'd him to her infant Son,
And taught his lisping tongue to name *Arsaces:*
E'en aged Sires, whose sounds are scarcely heard,
By feeble strength supported, tost their caps,
And gave their murmur to the gen'ral voice.

GOTARZES.

The spacious streets, which lead up to the Temple,
Are strew'd with flow'rs; each, with frantic joy,
His garland forms, and throws it in the way.
What pleasure, *Phraates*, must swell his bosom,
So see the prostrate nation all around him,
And know he's made them happy! to hear them
Tease the Gods, to show'r their blessings on him!
Happy *Arsaces!* fain I'd imitate
Thy matchless worth, and be a shining joy!

PHRAATES.

Hark! what a shout was that which pierc'd the skies!
It seem'd as tho' all Nature's beings join'd,
To hail thy glorious Brother.

GOTARZES.

Happy *Parthia!*
Now proud *Arabia* dreads her destin'd chains,

While shame and rout disperses all her sons.
Barzaphernes pursues the fugitives,
The few whom fav'ring Night redeem'd from slaughter;
Swiftly they fled, for fear had wing'd their speed,
And made them bless the shade which saf'ty gave.

PHRAATES.

What a bright hope is ours, when those dread pow'rs
Who rule yon heav'n, and guide the mov'ments here,
Shall call your royal Father to their joys:
In blest *Arsaces* ev'ry virtue meets;
He's gen'rous, brave, and wise, and good,
Has skill to act, and noble fortitude
To face bold danger, in the battle firm,
And dauntless as a Lion fronts his foe.
Yet is he sway'd by ev'ry tender passion,
Forgiving mercy, gentleness and love;
Which speak the Hero friend of humankind.

GOTARZES.

And let me speak, for 'tis to him I owe
That here I stand, and breath the common air,
And 'tis my pride to tell it to the world.
One luckless day as in the eager chace
My Courser wildly bore me from the rest,
A monst'rous Leopard from a bosky fen
Rush'd forth, and foaming lash'd the ground,
And fiercely ey'd me as his destin'd quarry.
My jav'lin swift I threw, but o'er his head
It erring pass'd, and harmless in the air
Spent all its force; my falchin then I seiz'd,

Advancing to attack my ireful foe,
When furiously the savage sprung upon me,
And tore me to the ground; my treach'rous blade
Above my hand snap'd short, and left me quite
Defenceless to his rage; *Arsaces* then,
Hearing the din, flew like some pitying pow'r,
And quickly freed me from the Monster's paws,
Drenching his bright lance in his spotted breast.

PHRAATES.

How diff'rent he from arrogant *Vardanes?*
That haughty Prince eyes with a stern contempt
All other Mortals, and with lofty mien
He treads the earth as tho' he were a God.
Nay, I believe that his ambitious soul,
Had it but pow'r to its licentious wishes,
Would dare dispute with Jove the rule of heav'n;
Like a Titanian son with giant insolence,
Match with the Gods, and wage immortal war,
'Til their red wrath should hurl him headlong down,
E'en to destruction's lowest pit of horror.

GOTARZES.

Methinks he wears not that becoming joy
Which on this bright occasion gilds the court;
His brow's contracted with a gloomy frown,
Pensive he stalks along, and seems a prey
To pining discontent.

PHRAATES.

Arsaces he dislikes,
For standing 'twixt him, and the hope of Empire;

While Envy, like a rav'nous Vulture tears
His canker'd heart, to see your Brother's triumph.

GOTARZES.

And yet *Vardanes* owes that hated Brother
As much as I; 'twas summer last, as we
Were bathing in *Euphrates'* flood, *Vardanes*
Proud of strength would seek the further shore;
But 'ere he the mid-stream gain'd, a poignant pain
Shot thro' his well-strung nerves, contracting all,
And the stiff joints refus'd their wonted aid.
Loudly he cry'd for help, *Arsaces* heard,
And thro' the swelling waves he rush'd to save
His drowning Brother, and gave him life,
And for the boon the Ingrate pays him hate.

PHRAATES.

There's something in the wind, for I've observ'd
Of late he much frequents the Queen's apartment,
And fain would court her favour, wild is she
To gain revenge for fell *Vonones'* death,
And firm resolves the ruin of *Arsaces.*
Because that fill'd with filial piety,
To save his Royal Sire, he struck the bold
Presumptuous Traitor dead; nor heeds she
The hand which gave her Liberty, nay rais'd her
Again to Royalty.

GOTARZES.

Ingratitude,
Thou hell-born fiend, how horrid is thy form!
The Gods sure let thee loose to scourge mankind,
And save them from an endless waste of thunder.

PHRAATES.

Yet I've beheld this now so haughty Queen,
Bent with distress, and e'en by pride forsook,
When following thy Sire's triumphant car,
Her tears and ravings mov'd the senseless herd,
And pity blest their more than savage breasts,
With the short pleasure of a moments softness.
Thy Father, conquer'd by her charms, (for what
Can charm like mourning beauty) soon struck off
Her chains, and rais'd her to his bed and throne.
Adorn'd the brows of her aspiring Son,
The fierce *Vonones,* with the regal crown
Of rich *Armenia,* once the happy rule
Of *Tisaphernes,* her deceased Lord.

GOTARZES.

And he in wasteful war return'd his thanks,
Refus'd the homage he had sworn to pay,
And spread Destruction ev'ry where around,
'Til from *Arsaces* hand he met the fate
His crimes deserv'd.

PHRAATES.

As yet your princely Brother
Has scap'd *Thermusa's* rage, for still residing
In peaceful times, within his Province, ne'er
Has fortune blest her with a sight of him,
On whom she'd wreck her vengeance.

GOTARZES.

She has won
By spells, I think, so much on my fond father,
That he is guided by her will alone.

She rules the realm, her pleasure is a law,
All offices and favours are bestow'd
As she directs.

PHRAATES.

But see, the Prince, *Vardanes,*
Proud *Lysias* with him, he whose soul is harsh
With jarring discord. Nought but madding rage,
And ruffian-like revenge his breast can know,
Indeed to gain a point he'll condescend
To mask the native rancour of his heart,
And smooth his venom'd tongue with flattery.
Assiduous now he courts *Vardanes'* friendship,
See, how he seems to answer all his gloom,
And give him frown for frown.

GOTARZES.

Let us retire,
And shun them now; I know not what it means,
But chilling horror shivers o'er my limbs,
When *Lysias* I behold.

SCENE II.

VARDANES AND LYSIAS.

LYSIAS.

That shout proclaims [Shout.
Arsaces near approach.

VARDANES.

Peace, prithee peace,
Wilt thou still shock me with that hated sound,

And grate harsh discord in my offended ear?
If thou art fond of echoing the name,
Join with the servile croud, and hail his triumph.

LYSIAS.

I hail him? By our glorious shining God,
I'd sooner lose my speech, and all my days
In silence rest, conversing with my thoughts,
Than hail *Arsaces.*

VARDANES.

Yet, again his name,
Sure there is magic in it, PARTHIA's drunk
And giddy with the joy; the houses tops
With gaping spectators are throng'd, nay wild
They climb such precipices that the eye
Is dazzl'd with their daring; ev'ry wretch
Who long has been immur'd, nor dar'd enjoy
The common benefits of sun and air,
Creeps from his lurking place; e'en feeble age,
Long to the sickly couch confin'd, stalks forth,
And with infectious breath assails the Gods.
O! curse the name, the idol of their joy.

LYSIAS.

And what's that name, that thus they should disturb
The ambient air, and weary gracious heav'n
With ceaseless bellowings? *Vardanes* sounds
With equal harmony, and suits as well
The loud repeated shouts of noisy joy.
Can he bid Chaos Nature's rule dissolve,
Can he deprive mankind of light and day,

And turn the Seasons from their destin'd course?
Say, can he do all this, and be a God?
If not, what is his matchless merit? What dares he,
Vardanes dares not? blush not, noble prince,
For praise is merit's due, and I will give it;
E'en mid the croud which waits thy Brother's smile,
I'd loud proclaim the merit of *Vardanes.*

VARDANES.

Forbear this warmth, your friendship urges far.
Yet know your love shall e'er retain a place
In my remembrance. There is something here —
(*Pointing to his breast*)
Another time and I will give thee all;
But now, no more. —

LYSIAS.

You may command my service,
I'm happy to obey. Of late your Brother
Delights in hind'ring my advancement,
And ev'ry boaster's rais'd above my merit,
Barzaphernes alone commands his ear,
His oracle in all.

VARDANES.

I hate *Arsaces*
Tho' he's my Mother's son, and churchmen say
There's something sacred in the name of Brother.
My soul endures him not, and he's the bane
Of all my hopes of greatness. Like the sun
He rules the day, and like the night's pale Queen,
My fainter beams are lost when he appears.
And this because he came into the world,

A moon or two before me: What's the diff'rence,
That he alone should shine in Empire's seat?
I am not apt to trumpet forth my praise,
Or highly name myself, but this I'll speak,
To him in ought, I'm not the least inferior.
Ambition, glorious fever! mark of Kings,
Gave me immortal thirst and rule of Empire.
Why lag'd my tardy soul, why droop'd the wing,
Nor forward springing, shot before his speed
To seize the prize? — 'Twas Empire — Oh! 'twas Empire —

LYSIAS.

Yes, I must think that of superior mould
Your soul was form'd, fit for a heav'nly state,
And left reluctant its sublime abode,
And painfully obey'd the dread command,
When Jove's controuling fate forc'd it below.
His soul was earthly, and it downward mov'd,
Swift as to the center of attraction.

VARDANES.

It might be so — But I've another cause
To hate this Brother, ev'ry way my rival;
In love as well as glory he's above me;
I dote on fair *Evanthe*, but the charmer
Disdains my ardent suit, like a miser
He treasures up her beauties to himself:
Thus is he form'd to give me torture ever. —
But hark, they've reach'd the Temple,
Didst thou observe the croud, their eagerness,
Each put the next aside to catch a look,
Himself was elbow'd out? — Curse, curse their zeal —

LYSIAS.

Stupid folly!

VARDANES.

I'll tell thee *Lysias*,
This many-headed monster multitude,
Unsteady is as giddy fortune's wheel,
As woman fickle, varying as the wind;
To day they this way course, the next they veer,
And shift another point, the next another.

LYSIAS.

Curiosity's another name for man,
The blazing meteor streaming thro' the air
Commands our wonder, and admiring eyes,
With eager gaze we trace the lucent path,
'Til spent at length it shrinks to native nothing,
While the bright stars which ever steady glow,
Unheeded shine, and bless the world below.

SCENE III.

QUEEN AND EDESSA.

QUEEN.

Oh! give me way, the haughty victor comes,
Surrounded by adoring multitudes,
On swelling tides of praise to heav'n they raise him;
To deck their idol, they rob the glorious beings
Of their splendor.

EDESSA.

My royal Lady,
Chace hence these passions.

QUEEN.

Peace, forever peace,
Have I not cause to hate this homicide?
'Twas by his cursed hand *Vonones* fell,
Yet fell not as became his gallant spirit,
Not by the warlike arm of chief renown'd,
But by a youth, ye Gods, a beardless stripling,
Stab'd by his dastard falchin from behind;
For well I know he fear'd to meet *Vonones*,
As princely warriors meet with open daring,
But shrunk amidst his guards, and gave him death,
When faint with wounds, and weary with the fight.

EDESSA.

With anguish I have heard his hapless fate,
And mourn'd in silence for the gallant Prince.

QUEEN.

Soft is thy nature, but alas! *Edessa*,
Thy heart's a stranger to a mother's sorrows,
To see the pride of all her wishes blasted;
Thy fancy cannot paint the storm of grief,
Despair and anguish, which my breast has known.
Oh! show'r, ye Gods, your torments on *Arsaces*,
Curs'd be the morn which dawn'd upon his birth.

EDESSA.

Yet, I entreat —

QUEEN.

Away! for I will curse —
O may he never know a father's fondness,
Or know it to his sorrow, may his hopes
Of joy be cut like mine, and his short life

Be one continu'd tempest; if he lives,
Let him be curs'd with jealousy and fear,
And vext with anguish of neglecting scorn;
May tort'ring hope present the flowing cup,
Then hasty snatch it from his eager thirst,
And when he dies base treach'ry be the means.

EDESSA.

Oh! calm your spirits.

QUEEN.

Yes, I'll now be calm,
Calm as the sea when the rude waves are laid,
And nothing but a gentle swell remains;
My curse is heard, and I shall have revenge:
There's something here which tells me 'twill be so,
And peace resumes her empire o'er my breast.
Vardanes is the Minister of Vengeance;
Fir'd by ambition, he aspiring seeks
T' adorn his brows with *Parthia's* diadem;
I've fann'd the fire, and wrought him up to fury,
Envy shall urge him forward still to dare,
And discord be the prelude to destruction,
Then this detested race shall feel my hate.

EDESSA.

And doth thy hatred then extend so far,
That innocent and guilty all alike
Must feel thy dreadful vengeance?

QUEEN.

Ah! *Edessa,*
Thou dost not know e'en half my mighty wrongs,
But in thy bosom I will pour my sorrows.

EDESSA.

With secrecy I ever have repaid
Your confidence.

QUEEN.

I know thou hast, then hear,
The changeling King who oft has kneel'd before me,
And own'd no other pow'r, now treats me
With ill dissembl'd love mix'd with disdain.
A newer beauty rules his faithless heart,
Which only in variety is blest;
Oft have I heard him, when wrapt up in sleep,
And wanton fancy rais'd the mimic scene,
Call with unusual fondness on *Evanthe*,
While I have lain neglected by his side,
Except sometimes in a mistaken rapture
He'd clasp me to his bosom.

EDESSA.

Oh! Madam.
Let not corroding jealousy usurp
Your Royal breast, unnumber'd ills attend
The wretch who entertains that fatal guest.

QUEEN.

Think not that I'll pursue its wandring fires,
No more I'll know perplexing doubts and fears,
And erring trace suspicion's endless maze,
For, ah! I doubt no more.

EDESSA.

Their shouts approach.

QUEEN.

Lead me, *Edessa*, to some peaceful gloom,
Some silent shade far from the walks of men,
There shall the hop'd revenge my thoughts employ,
And sooth my sorrows with the coming joy.

SCENE IV.

EVANTHE AND CLEONE.

EVANTHE.

No I'll not meet him now, for love delights
In the soft pleasures of the secret shade,
And shuns the noise and tumult of the croud.
How tedious are the hours which bring him
To my fond panting heart ! for oh ! to those
Who live in expectation of the bliss,
Time slowly creeps, and ev'ry tardy minute,
Seems mocking of their wishes. Say, *Cleone*,
For you beheld the triumph, midst his pomp,
Did he not seem to curse the empty show,
The pageant greatness, enemy to love,
Which held him from *Evanthe?* haste, to tell me,
And feed my gready ear with the fond tale —
Yet, hold — for I shall weary you with questions,
And ne'er be satisfied — Beware, *Cleone*,
And guard your heart from Love's delusive sweets.

CLEONE.

Is Love an ill, that thus you caution me
To shun his pow'r?

EVANTHE.

The Tyrant, my *Cleone*,
Despotic rules, and fetters all our thoughts.
Oh! wouldst thou love, then bid adieu to peace,
Then fears will come, and jealousies intrude,
Ravage your bosom, and disturb your quiet,
E'en pleasure to excess will be a pain.
Once I was free, then my exulting heart
Was like a bird that hops from spray to spray,
And all was innocence and mirth; but, lo!
The Fowler came, and by his arts decoy'd,
And soon the Wanton cag'd. Twice fifteen times
Has *Cynthia* dipt her horns in beams of light,
Twice fifteen times has wasted all her brightness,
Since first I knew to love; 'twas on that day
When curs'd *Vonones* fell upon the plain,
The lovely Victor doubly conquer'd me.

CLEONE.

Forgive my boldness, Madam, if I ask
What chance first gave you to *Vonones*' pow'r?
Curiosity thou know'st is of our sex.

EVANTHE.

That is a task will wake me to new sorrows,
Yet thou attend, and I will tell thee all,
Arabia gave me birth, my father held
Great Offices at Court, and was reputed
Brave, wise and loyal, by his Prince belov'd.
Oft has he led his conqu'ring troops, and forc'd
From frowning victory her awful honours.
In infancy I was his only treasure,

On me he wasted all his store of fondness.
Oh ! I could tell thee of his wond'rous goodness,
His more than father's love and tenderness.
But thou wouldst jeer, and say the tale was trifling;
So did he dote upon me, for in childhood
My infant charms, and artless innocence
Blest his fond age, and won on ev'ry heart.
But, oh ! from this sprung ev'ry future ill,
This fatal beauty was the source of all.

CLEONE.

'Tis often so, for beauty is a flow'r
That tempts the hand to pluck it.

EVANTHE.

Full three times
Has scorching summer fled from cold winter's
Ruthless blasts, as oft again has spring
In sprightly youth drest nature in her beauties,
Since bathing in *Niphates'* [1] silver stream,
Attended only by one fav'rite maid;
As we were sporting on the wanton waves,
Swift from the wood a troop of horsemen rush'd,
Rudely they seiz'd, and bore me trembling off,
In vain *Edessa* with her shrieks assail'd
The heav'ns, for heav'n was deaf to both our pray'rs.
The wretch whose insolent embrace confin'd me,
(Like thunder bursting on the guilty soul)
With curs'd *Vonones* voice pour'd in my ears
A hateful tale of love; for he it seems

[1] The Tigris.

Had seen me at Arabia's royal court,
And took those means to force me to his arms.

CLEONE.

Perhaps you may gain something from the Captives
Of your lost Parents.

EVANTHE.

This I mean to try,
Soon as the night hides Nature in her darkness,
Veil'd in the gloom we'll steal into their prison.
But, oh ! perhaps e'en now my aged Sire
May 'mongst the slain lie weltering on the field,
Pierc'd like a riddle through with num'rous wounds,
While parting life is quiv'ring on his lips,
He may perhaps be calling on his *Evanthe.*
Yes, ye great Pow'rs who boast the name of mercy,
Ye have deny'd me to his latest moments,
To all the offices of filial duty,
To bind his wounds, and wash them with my tears,
Is this, is this your mercy?

CLEONE.

Blame not heav'n,
For heav'n is just and kind; dear Lady drive
These black ideas from your gentle breast;
Fancy delights to torture the distress'd,
And fill the gloomy scene with shadowy ills,
Summon your reason, and you'll soon have comfort.

EVANTHE.

Dost thou name comfort to me, my *Cleone,*
Thou who know'st all my sorrows? plead no more,
'Tis reason tells me I am doubly wretched.

CLEONE.

But hark, the music strikes, the rites begin,
And, see, the doors are op'ning.

EVANTHE.

Let's retire;
My heart is now too full to meet him here,
Fly swift ye hours, till in his arms I'm prest,
And each intruding care is hush'd to rest.

SCENE V.

The Scene draws and discovers, in the inner Part of the Temple, a large Image of the Sun, with an Altar before it. Around Priests and Attendants.

KING, ARSACES, VARDANES, GOTARZES, PHRAATES, LYSIAS, with BETHAS in chains.

HYMN.

Parent of Light, to thee belong
Our grateful tributary songs;
Each thankful voice to thee shall rise,
And chearful pierce the azure skies;
While in thy praise all earth combines,
And Echo in the Chorus joins.

All the gay pride of blooming May,
The Lily fair and blushing Rose,
To thee their early honours pay,
And all their heav'nly sweets disclose.

The feather'd Choir on ev'ry tree
 To hail thy glorious dawn repair,
While the sweet sons of harmony
 With Hallelujah's fill the air.

'Tis thou hast brac'd the Hero's arm,
And giv'n the Love of praise to warm
His bosom, as he onward flies,
And for his Country bravely dies.
Thine's victory, and from thee springs
Ambition's fire, which glows in Kings.

KING. (Coming forward)

Thus, to the Gods our tributary songs,
And now, oh! let me welcome once again
My blooming victor to his Father's arms;
And let me thank thee for our safety: PARTHIA
Shall thank thee too, and give her grateful praise
To her Deliverer.

OMNES.

All hail! *Arsaces!*

KING.

Thanks to my loyal friends.

VARDANES. (Aside)

Curse, curse the sound,
E'en Echo gives it back with int'rest,
The joyful gales swell with the pleasing theme,
And waft it far away to distant hills.
O that my breath was poison, then indeed
I'd hail him like the rest, but blast him too.

ARSACES.

My Royal Sire, these honours are unmerited,
Beneath your prosp'rous auspices I fought,
Bright vict'ry to your banners joyful flew,
And favour'd for the Sire the happy son.
But lenity should grace the victor's laurels,
Then, here, my gracious Father —

KING.

Ha ! 'tis *Bethas !*
Know'st thou, vain wretch, what fate attends on those
Who dare oppose the pow'r of mighty Kings,
Whom heav'n delights to favour? sure some God
Who fought to punish you for impious deeds,
'Twas urg'd you forward to insult our arms,
And brave us at our Royal City's gates.

BETHAS.

At honour's call, and at my King's command,
Tho' it were even with my single arm, again
I'd brave the multitude, which, like a deluge,
O'erwhelm'd my gallant handful; yea wou'd meet
Undaunted, all the fury of the torrent.
'Tis honour is the guide of all my actions,
The ruling star by which I steer thro' life,
And shun the shelves of infamy and vice.

KING.

It was the thrift of gain which drew you on;
'Tis thus that Av'rice always cloaks its views,
Th' ambition of your Prince you gladly snatch'd

As opportunity to fill your coffers.
It was the plunder of our palaces,
And of our wealthy cities, fill'd your dreams,
And urg'd you on your way; but you have met
The due reward of your audacity.
Now shake your chains, shake and delight your ears
With the soft music of your golden fetters.

BETHAS.

True, I am fall'n, but glorious was my fall,
The day was brav'ly fought, we did our best,
But victory's of heav'n. Look o'er yon field,
See if thou findest one *Arabian* back
Disfigur'd with dishonourable wounds.
No, here, deep on their bosoms, are engrav'd
The marks of honour! 'twas thro' here their souls
Flew to their blissful seats. Oh! why did I
Survive the fatal day? To be this slave,
To be the gaze and sport of vulgar crouds,
Thus, like a shackl'd tyger, stalk my round,
And grimly low'r upon the shouting herd.
Ye Gods! —

KING.

Away with him to instant death.

ARSACES.

Hear me, my Lord, O, not on this bright day,
Let not this day of joy blush with his blood.
Nor count his steady loyalty a crime,
But give him life, *Arsaces* humbly asks it,
And may you e'er be serv'd with honest hearts.

KING.

Well, be it so; hence, bear him to his dungeon;
Lysias, we here commit him to thy charge.

BETHAS.

Welcome my dungeon, but more welcome death.
Trust not too much, vain Monarch, to your pow'r,
Know fortune places all her choicest gifts
On ticklish heights, they shake with ev'ry breeze,
And oft some rude wind hurls them to the ground.
Jove's thunder strikes the lofty palaces,
While the low cottage, in humility,
Securely stands, and sees the mighty ruin.
What King can boast, to morrow as to day,
Thus, happy will I reign? The rising sun
May view him seated on a splendid throne,
And, setting, see him shake the servile chain.
[Exit guarded.

SCENE VI.

KING, ARSACES, VARDANES, GOTARZES, PHRAATES.

GOTARZES.

Thus let me hail thee from the croud distinct,
For in the exulting voice of gen'ral joy
My fainter sounds were lost, believe me, Brother,
My soul dilates with joy to see thee thus.

ARSACES.

Thus let me thank thee in this fond embrace.

VARDANES.

The next will be my turn, Gods, I had rather
Be circl'd in a venom'd serpent's fold.

GOTARZES.

O, my lov'd Brother, 'tis my humble boon,
That, when the war next calls you to the field,
I may attend you in the rage of battle.
By imitating thy heroic deeds,
Perhaps, I may rise to some little worth,
Beneath thy care I'll try my feeble wings,
Till taught by thee to soar to nobler heights.

KING.

Why that's my boy, thy spirit speaks thy birth,
No more I'll turn thee from the road to glory,
To rust in slothfulness, with lazy Gownsmen.

GOTARZES.

Thanks, to my Sire, I'm now completely blest.

ARSACES.

But, I've another Brother, where's *Vardanes?*

KING.

Ha! what, methinks, he lurks behind the croud,
And wears a gloom which suits not with the time.

VARDANES.

Doubt not my Love, tho' I lack eloquence,
To dress my sentiments and catch the ear,
Tho' plain my manners, and my language rude,

My honest heart disdains to wear disguise.
Then think not I am slothful in the race,
Or, that my Brother springs before my Love.

ARSACES.

Far be suspicion from me.

VARDANES.

So, 'tis done,
Thanks to dissembling, all is well again.

KING.

Now let us, forward, to the Temple go,
And let, with chearful wine, the goblets flow;
Let blink-ey'd Jollity his aid afford,
To crown our triumph, round the festive board:
But, let the wretch, whose soul can know a care,
Far from our joys, to some lone shade repair,
In secrecy, there let him e'er remain,
Brood o'er his gloom, and still increase his pain.

END of the First *ACT*.

ACT II. SCENE I.

A PRISON.

LYSIAS, *alone.*

The Sun set frowning, and refreshing Eve
Lost all its sweets, obscur'd in double gloom.
This night shall sleep be stranger to these eyes,
Peace dwells not here, and slumber flies the shock;
My spirits, like the elements, are waring,
And mock the tempest with a kindred rage —
I, who can joy in nothing, but revenge,
Know not those boasted ties of Love and Friendship;
Vardanes I regard, but as he gives me
Some hopes of vengeance on the Prince *Arsaces* —
But, ha! he comes, wak'd by the angry storm,
'Tis to my wish, thus would I form designs,
Horror should breed beneath the veil of horror,
And darkness aid conspiracies — He's here —

SCENE II.

VARDANES and LYSIAS.

LYSIAS.

Welcome, my noble Prince,

VARDANES.

Thanks, gentle friend;

Heav'ns! what a night is this!

LYSIAS.

'Tis fill'd with terror;
Some dread event beneath this horror lurks,
Ordain'd by fate's irrevocable doom;
Perhaps *Arsaces*' fall — and angry heav'n
Speaks it, in thunder, to the trembling world.

VARDANES.

Terror indeed! it seems as sick'ning Nature
Had giv'n her order up to gen'ral ruin;
The Heav'ns appear as one continu'd flame,
Earth with her terror shakes, dim night retires,
And the red lightning gives a dreadful day,
While in the thunder's voice each sound is lost;
Fear sinks the panting heart in ev'ry bosom,
E'en the pale dead, affrighted at the horror,
As tho' unsafe, start from their marble goals,
And howling thro' the streets are seeking shelter.

LYSIAS.

I saw a flash stream thro' the angry clouds,
And bend its course to where a stately pine
Behind the garden stood, quickly it seiz'd,
And wrapt it in a fiery fold, the trunk
Was shiver'd into atoms, and the branches
Off were lopt, and wildly scatter'd round.

VARDANES.

Why rage the elements, they are not curs'd
Like me? *Evanthe* frowns not angry on them,
The wind may play upon her beauteous bosom
Nor fear her chiding, light can bless her sense,

And in the floating mirror she beholds
Those beauties which can fetter all mankind.
Earth gives her joy, she plucks the fragrant rose,
Pleas'd takes its sweets, and gazes on its bloom.

LYSIAS.

My Lord, forget her, tear her from your breast.
Who, like the *Phœnix*, gazes on the sun,
And strives to soar up to the glorious blaze,
Should never leave Ambition's brightest object,
To turn, and view the beauties of a flow'r.

VARDANES.

O, Lysias, chide no more, for, I have done.
Yes, I'll forget this proud disdainful beauty;
Hence, with, vain love — Ambition, now, alone,
Shall guide my actions, since mankind delights
To give me pain, I'll study mischief too,
And shake the earth, e'en like this raging tempest.

LYSIAS.

A night like this, so dreadful to behold,
Since my remembrance's birth, I never saw.

VARDANES.

E'en such a night, dreadful as this, they say,
My teeming Mother gave me to the world.
Whence by those sages who, in knowledge rich,
Can pry into futurity, and tell
What distant ages will produce of wonder,
My days were deemed to be a hurricane;
My early life prov'd their prediction false;
Beneath a sky serene my voyage began,

But, to this long uninterrupted calm,
Storms shall succeed.

LYSIAS.

Then haste, to raise the tempest;
My soul disdains this one eternal round,
Where each succeeding day is like the former.
Trust me, my noble Prince, here is a heart
Steady and firm to all your purposes,
And here's a hand that knows to execute
Whate'er designs thy daring breast can form,
Nor ever shake with fear.

VARDANES.

And I will use it,
Come to my bosom, let me place thee here,
How happy am I clasping so much virtue!
Now, by the light, it is my firm belief,
One mighty soul in common swells our bosoms,
Such sameness can't be matched in diff'rent beings.

LYSIAS.

Your confidence, my Lord, much honours me,
And when I act unworthy of your love
May I be hooted from Society,
As tho' disgraceful to the human kind,
And driv'n to herd among the savage race.

VARDANES.

Believe me, *Lysias*, I do not know
A single thought which tends toward suspicion,
For well I know thy worth, when I affront it,
By the least doubt, may I be ever curs'd

With faithless friends, and by his dagger fall
Whom my deluded wishes most would favour.

LYSIAS.

Then let's no longer trifle time away,
I'm all impatience till I see thy brows
Bright in the glories of a diadem;
My soul is fill'd with anguish when I think
That by weak Princes worn, 'tis thus disgrac'd.
Haste, mount the throne, and, like the morning Sun,
Chace with your piercing beams those mists away,
Which dim the glory of the *Parthian* state:
Each honest heart desires it, numbers there are
Ready to join you, and support your cause,
Against th' opposing faction.

VARDANES.

Sure some God,
Bid you thus call me to my dawning honours,
And joyful I obey the pleasing summons.
Now by the pow'rs of heav'n, of earth and hell,
Most solemnly I swear, I will not know
That quietude which I was wont to know,
'Til I have climb'd the height of all my wishes,
Or fell, from glory, to the silent grave.

LYSIAS.

Nobly resolv'd, and spoken like *Vardanes*,
There shone my Prince in his superior lustre.

VARDANES.

But then, *Arsaces*, he's a fatal bar —
O! could I brush this busy insect from me,

Which envious strives to rob me of my bloom,
Then might I, like some fragrant op'ning flow'r,
Spread all my beauties in the face of day.
Ye Gods! why did ye give me such a soul,
(A soul, which ev'ry way is form'd for Empire)
And damn me with a younger Brother's right?
The diadem would set as well on mine,
As on the brows of any lordly He;
Nor is this hand weak to enforce command.
And shall I steal into my grave, and give
My name up to oblivion, to be thrown
Among the common rubbish of the times?
No: Perish first, this happy hated Brother.

LYSIAS.

I always wear a dagger, for your service,
I need not speak the rest —
When humbly I intreated of your Brother
T'attend him as Lieutenant in this war,
Frowning contempt, he haughtily reply'd,
He entertain'd not Traitors in his service.
True, I betray'd *Orodes*, but with cause,
He struck me, like a sorry abject slave,
And still withheld from giving what he'd promis'd.
Fear not *Arsaces*, believe me, he shall
Soon his Quietus have — But, see, he comes, —
What can this mean? Why at this lonely hour,
And unattended? — Ha! 'tis opportune —
I'll in, and stab him now. I heed not what
The danger is, so I but have revenge,
Then heap perdition on me.

VARDANES.

Hold, awhile —
'Twould be better could we undermine him,
And make him fall by *Artabanus*' doom.

LYSIAS.

Well, be it so —

VARDANES.

But let us now retire,
We must not be observ'd together here.

SCENE III.

ARSACES, *alone.*

'Tis here that hapless *Bethas* is confin'd;
He who, but yesterday, like angry Jove,
When punishing the crimes of guilty men,
Spread death and desolation all around,
While PARTHIA trembl'd at his name; is now
Unfriended and forlorn, and counts the hours,
Wrapt in the gloomy horrors of a gaol. —
How dark, and hidden, are the turns of fate!
His rigid fortune moves me to compassion.
O! 'tis a heav'nly virtue when the heart
Can feel the sorrows of another's bosom,
It dignifies the man: The stupid wretch
Who knows not this sensation, is an image,
And wants the feeling to make up a life —
I'll in, and give my aid to sooth his sorrows.

SCENE IV.

VARDANES and LYSIAS.

LYSIAS.

Let us observe with care, something we, yet,
May gather, to give to us the vantage;
No matter what's the intent.

VARDANES.

How easy 'tis
To cheat this busy, tattling, censuring world!
For fame still names our actions, good or bad,
As introduc'd by chance, which ofttimes throws
Wrong lights on objects; vice she dresses up
In the bright form, and goodliness, of virtue,
While virtue languishes, and pines neglected,
Rob'd of her lustre — But, let's forward *Lysias* —
Thou know'st each turn in this thy dreary rule,
Then lead me to some secret stand, from whence,
Unnotic'd, all their actions we may view.

LYSIAS.

Here, take your stand behind — See, *Bethas* comes.
(They retire)

SCENE V.

BETHAS, alone.

To think on Death, in gloomy solitude,
In dungeons and in chains, when expectation

Join'd with serious thought describe him to us,
His height'n'd terrors strike upon the soul
With awful dread; imagination rais'd
To frenzy, plunges in a sea of horror,
And tastes the pains, the agonies of dying —
Ha ! who is this, perhaps he bears my fate?
It must be so, but, why this privacy?

SCENE VI.

ARSACES and BETHAS.

ARSACES.

Health to the noble *Bethas*, health and joy !

BETHAS.

A steady harden'd villain, one experienc'd
In his employment; ha ! where's thy dagger?
It cannot give me fear; I'm ready, see,
My op'ning bosom tempts the friendly steel.
Fain would I cast this tiresome being off,
Like an old garment worn to wretchedness.
Here, strike for I'm prepar'd.

ARSACES.

Oh ! view me better,
Say, do I wear the gloomy ruffian's frown?

BETHAS.

Ha ! 'tis the gallant Prince, the brave *Arsaces*,
And *Bethas*' Conqueror.

ARSACES.

And *Bethas'* friend,
A name I'm proud to wear.

BETHAS.

Away — away —
Mock with your jester to divert the court,
Fit Scene for sportive joys and frolic mirth;
Thinkst thou I lack that manly constancy
Which braves misfortune, and remains unshaken?
Are these, are these the emblems of thy friendship,
These rankling chains, say, does it gall like these?
No, let me taste the bitterness of sorrow,
For I am reconcil'd to wretchedness.
The Gods have empty'd all their mighty store,
Of hoarded Ills, upon my whiten'd age;
Now death — but, oh! I court coy death in vain,
Like a cold maid, he scorns my fond complaining.
'Tis thou, insulting Prince, 'tis thou hast dragg'd
My soul, just rising, down again to earth,
And clogg'd her wings with dull mortality,
A hateful bondage! Why —

ARSACES.

A moment hear me —

BETHAS.

Why dost thou, like an angry vengeful ghost,
Glide hither to disturb this peaceful gloom?
What, dost thou envy me my miseries,
My chains and flinty pavement, where I oft
In sleep behold the image of the death I wish,

Forget my sorrows and heart-breaking anguish?
These horrors I would undisturb'd enjoy,
Attended only by my silent thoughts;
Is it to see the wretch that you have made,
To view the ruins of unhappy *Bethas*,
And triumph in my grief? Is it for this
You penetrate my dark joyless prison?

ARSACES.

Oh! do not injure me by such suspicions.
Unknown to me are cruel scoffs and jests;
My breast can feel compassion's tenderness,
The warrior's warmth, the soothing joys of friendship.
When adverse bold battalions shook the earth,
And horror triumph'd on the hostile field,
I fought you with a glorious enmity,
And arm'd my brow with the stern frown of war.
But now the angry trumpet wakes no more
The youthful champion to the lust for blood.
Retiring rage gives place to softer passions,
And gen'rous warriors know no longer hate,
The name of foe is lost, and thus I ask
Your friendship.

BETHAS.

Ah! why dost thou mock me thus!

ARSACES.

Let the base coward, he who ever shrinks,
And trembles, at the slight name of danger,
Taunt, and revile, with bitter gibes, the wretched;
The brave are ever to distress a friend.

Tho' my dear country, (spoil'd by wasteful war,
Her harvests blazing, desolate her towns,
And baleful ruin shew'd her hagard face)
Call'd out on me to save her from her foes,
And I obey'd, yet to your gallant prowess,
And unmatch'd deeds, I admiration gave.
But now my country knows the sweets of safety,
Freed from her fears; sure now I may indulge
My just esteem for your superior virtue.

BETHAS.

Yes, I must think you what you would be thought,
For honest minds are easy of belief,
And always judge of others by themselves,
But often are deceiv'd; yet *Parthia* breeds not
Virtue much like thine, the barb'rous clime teems
With nought else but villains vers'd in ill.

ARSACES.

Dissimulation never mark'd my looks,
Nor flatt'ring deceit e'er taught my tongue,
The tale of falsehood, to disguise my thoughts:
To Virtue, and, her fair companion, Truth,
I've ever bow'd, their holy precepts kept,
And scann'd by them the actions of my life.
Suspicion surely ne'er disturbs the brave,
They never know the fears of doubting thoughts;
But free, as are the altars of the Gods,
From ev'ry hand receive the sacrifice.

SCENE VII.

ARSACES, BETHAS, EVANTHE and CLEONE.

EVANTHE.

Heav'ns! what a gloom hangs round this dreadful
place,
Fit habitation for the guilty mind!
Oh! if such terrors wait the innocent,
Which tread these vaults, what must the impious feel,
Who've all their crimes to stare them in the face?

BETHAS.

Immortal Gods! is this reality?
Or meer illusion? am I blest at last,
Or is it to torment me that you've rais'd
This semblance of *Evanthe* to my eyes?
It is! it is! 'tis she! —

ARSACES.

Ha! — what means this? —
She faints! she faints! life has forsook its seat,
Pale Death usurps its place — *Evanthe,* Oh!
Awake to life! — Love and *Arsaces* call! —

BETHAS.

Off — give her to my arms, my warm embrace
Shall melt Death's icy chains.

CLEONE.

She lives! she lives! —
See, on her cheeks the rosy glow returns.

ARSACES.

O joy! O joy! her op'ning eyes, again,
Break, like the morning sun, a better day.

BETHAS.

Evanthe! —

EVANTHE.

Oh! my Father! —

ARSACES.

Ha! — her Father!

BETHAS.

Heav'n thou art kind at last, and this indeed
Is recompense for all the ills I've past;
For all the sorrows which my heart has known,
Each wakeful night, and ev'ry day of anguish.
This, this has sweet'n'd all my bitter cup,
And gave me once again to taste of joy,
Joy which has long been stranger to this bosom.
Hence — hence disgrace — off, ignominy off —
But one embrace — I ask but one embrace,
And 'tis deny'd.

EVANTHE.

O, yes, around thy neck
I'll fold my longing arms, thy softer fetters,
Thus press thee to my happy breast, and kiss
Away those tears that stain thy aged cheeks.

BETHAS.

Oh! 'tis too much! it is too much! ye Gods!
Life's at her utmost stretch, and bursting near
With heart-swoln ecstasy; now let me die.

ARSACES.

What marble heart
Could see this scene unmov'd, nor give a tear?
My eyes grow dim, and sympathetic passion
Falls like a gushing torrent on my bosom.

EVANTHE.

O! happy me, this place, which lately seem'd
So fill'd with horror, now is pleasure's circle.
Here will I fix my seat; my pleasing task
Shall be to cherish thy remaining life.
All night I'll keep a vigil o'er thy slumbers,
And on my breast repose thee, mark thy dreams,
And when thou wak'st invent some pleasing tale,
Or with my songs the tedious hours beguile.

BETHAS.

Still let me gaze, still let me gaze upon thee,
Let me strain ev'ry nerve with ravishment,
And all my life be center'd in my vision.
To see thee thus, to hear thy angel voice,
It is, indeed, a luxury of pleasure! —
Speak, speak again, for oh! 'tis heav'n to hear thee!
Celestial sweetness dwells on ev'ry accent; —
Lull me to rest, and sooth my raging joy.
Joy which distracts me with unruly transports.
Now, by thy dear departed Mother's shade,
Thou brightest pattern of all excellence,
Thou who in prattling infancy hast blest me,
I wou'd not give this one transporting moment,
This fullness of delight, for all — but, ah!
'Tis vile, Ambition, Glory, all is vile,
To the soft sweets of love and tenderness.

EVANTHE.

Now let me speak, my throbbing heart is full,
I'll tell thee all — alas ! I have forgot —
'T'as slipt me in the tumult of my joy.
And yet I thought that I had much to say.

BETHAS.

Oh ! I have curs'd my birth, indeed, I have
Blasphem'd the Gods, with unbecoming passion,
Arraign'd their Justice, and defy'd their pow'r,
In bitterness, because they had deny'd
Thee to support the weakness of my age.
But now no more I'll rail and rave at fate,
All its decrees are just, complaints are impious,
Whate'er short-sighted mortals feel, springs from
Their blindness in the ways of Providence;
Sufficient wisdom 'tis for man to know
That the great Ruler is e'er wise and good.

ARSACES.

Ye figur'd stones !
Ye senseless, lifeless images of men,
Who never gave a tear to others woe,
Whose bosoms never glow'd for others good,
O weary heav'n with your repeated pray'rs,
And strive to melt the angry pow'rs to pity,
That ye may truly live.

EVANTHE.

Oh ! how my heart
Beats in my breast, and shakes my trembling frame !
I sink beneath this sudden flood of joy,
Too mighty for my spirits.

ARSACES.

My *Evanthe*.
Thus in my arms I catch thy falling beauties,
Chear thee; and kiss thee back to life again:
Thus to my bosom I could ever hold thee,
And find new pleasure.

EVANTHE,

O! my lov'd, *Arsaces*,
Forgive me that I saw thee not before,
Indeed my soul was busily employ'd,
Nor left a single thought at liberty.
But thou, I know, art gentleness and love.
Now I am double paid for all my sorrows,
For all my fears for thee.

ARSACES.

Then, fear no more:
Give to guilty wretches painful terrors:
Whose keen remembrance raises horrid forms,
Shapes that in spite of nature shock their souls
With dreadful anguish: but thy gentle bosom,
Whose innocence beams light and gayety,
Can never know a fear, now shining joy
Shall gild the pleasing scene.

EVANTHE.

Alas! this joy
I fear is like a sudden flame shot from
Th' expiring taper, darkness will ensue,
And double night I dread enclose us round.
Anxiety does yet disturb my breast,
And frightful apprehension shakes my soul.

BETHAS.

How shall I thank you, ye bright glorious beings!
Shall I in humble adoration bow,
Or fill the earth with your resounding praise?
No, this I leave to noisy hypocrites,
A Mortal's tongue disgraces such a theme;
But heav'n delights where silent gratitude
Mounts each aspiring thought to its bright throne,
Nor leaves to language aught; words may indeed
From man to man their sev'ral wants express,
Heav'n asks the purer incense of the heart.

ARSACES.

I'll to the King, 'ere he retires to rest,
Nor will I leave him 'til I've gain'd your freedom;
His love will surely not deny me this.

SCENE VIII.

VARDANES and LYSIAS (come forward)

LYSIAS.

'Twas a moving Scene, e'en my rough nature
Was nighly melted.

VARDANES.

Hence coward pity —
What is joy to them, to me is torture.
Now am I rack'd with pains that far exceed
Those agonies, which fabling Priests relate,
The damn'd endure: The shock of hopeless Love,

Unblest with any views to sooth ambition,
Rob me of all my reas'ning faculties.
Arsaces gains *Evanthe,* fills the throne,
While I am doom'd to foul obscurity,
To pine and grieve neglected.

LYSIAS.

My noble Prince,
Would it not be a master-piece, indeed,
To make this very bliss their greatest ill,
And damn them in the very folds of joy?

VARDANES.

This I will try, and stretch my utmost art,
Unknown is yet the means — We'll think on that —
Success may follow if you'll lend your aid.

LYSIAS.

The storm still rages — I must to the King,
And know what further orders 'ere he sleeps:
Soon I'll return, and speak my mind more fully.

VARDANES.

Haste, *Lysias*, haste, to aid me with thy council;
For without thee, all my designs will prove
Like night and chaos, darkness and confusion;
But to thy word shall light and order spring. —
Let coward Schoolmen talk of Virtue's rules,
And preach the vain Philosophy of fools;
Court eager their obscurity, afraid
To taste a joy, and in some gloomy shade

Dream o'er their lives, while in a mournful strain
They sing of happiness, they never gain.
But form'd for nobler purposes I come,
To gain a crown, or else a glorious tomb.

END of the SECOND *ACT*.

ACT III. — SCENE I.

The PALACE.

QUEEN and EDESSA.

QUEEN.

Talk not of sleep to me, the God of Rest
Disdains to visit where disorder reigns;
Not beds of down, nor music's softest strains,
Can charm him when 'tis anarchy within.
He flies with eager haste the mind disturb'd,
And sheds his blessings where the soul's in peace.

EDESSA.

Yet, hear me, Madam!

QUEEN.

Hence, away, *Edessa,*
For thou know'st not the pangs of jealousy.
Say, has he not forsook my bed, and left me
Like a lone widow mourning to the night?
This, with the injury his son has done me,
If I forgive, may heav'n in anger show'r
Its torments on me — Ha! isn't that the King?

EDESSA.

It is your Royal Lord, great *Artabanus.*

QUEEN.

Leave me, for I would meet him here alone,
Something is lab'ring in my breast —

SCENE II.

KING and QUEEN.

KING.

This leads
To fair *Evanthe's* chamber — Ha ! the Queen.

QUEEN.

Why dost thou start ? so starts the guilty wretch,
When, by some watchful eye, prevented from
His dark designs.

KING.

Prevented ! how, what mean'st thou ?

QUEEN.

Art thou then so dull ? cannot thy heart,
Thy changeling heart, explain my meaning to thee,
Or must upbraiding 'wake thy apprehension ?
Ah ! faithless, tell me, have I lost those charms
Which thou so oft hast sworn could warm old age,
And tempt the frozen hermit from his cell,
To visit once again our gayer world ?
This, thou hast sworn, perfidious as thou art,
A thousand times ; as often hast thou sworn
Eternal constancy, and endless love,
Yet ev'ry time was perjur'd.

KING.

Sure, 'tis frenzy.

QUEEN.

Indeed, 'tis frenzy, 'tis the height of madness,
For I have wander'd long in sweet delusion,
At length the pleasing Phantom chang'd its form,
And left me in a wilderness of woe.

KING.

Prithee, no more, dismiss those jealous heats;
Love must decay, and soon disgust arise,
Where endless jarrings and upbraidings damp
The gentle flame, which warms the lover's breast.

QUEEN.

Oh! grant me patience heav'n! and dost thou think
By these reproaches to disguise thy guilt?
No, 'tis in vain, thy art's too thin to hide it.

KING.

Curse on the marriage chain! — the clog, a wife,
Who still will force and pall us with the joy,
Tho' pow'r is wanting, and the will is cloy'd,
Still urge the debt when Nothing's left to pay.

QUEEN.

Ha! dost thou own thy crime, nor feel the glow
Of conscious shame?

KING.

Why should I blush, if heav'n
Has made me as I am, and gave me passions?

Blest only in variety, then blame
The Gods, who form'd my nature thus, not me.

QUEEN.

Oh! Traitor! Villain!

KING.

Hence — away —
No more I'll wage a woman's war with words. (Exit)

QUEEN.

Down, down ye rising passions, give me ease,
Or break my heart, for I must yet be calm —
But, yet, revenge, our Sex's joy, is mine;
By all the Gods! he lives not till the morn.
Who slights my love, shall sink beneath my hate.

SCENE III.

QUEEN and VARDANES.

VARDANES.

What, raging to the tempest?

QUEEN.

Away! — away! —
Yes, I will rage — a tempest's here within,
Above the trifling of the noisy elements.
Blow ye loud winds, burst with your violence,
For ye but barely imitate the storm
That wildly rages in my tortur'd breast —
The King — the King —

VARDANES.

Ha! what? — the King?

QUEEN.

Evanthe! —

VARDANES.

You talk like riddles, still obscure and short,
Give me some cue to guide me thro' this maze.

QUEEN.

Ye pitying pow'rs! — oh! for a poison, some
Curs'd deadly draught, that I might blast her beauties,
And rob her eyes of all their fatal lustre.

VARDANES.

What, blast her charms? — dare not think of it —
Shocking impiety; — the num'rous systems
Which gay creation spreads, bright blazing suns,
With all th' attendant planets circling round,
Are not worth half the radiance of her eyes.
She's heav'n's peculiar care, good spir'ts hover
Round, a shining band, to guard her beauties.

QUEEN.

Be they watchful then; for should remissness
Taint the guard, I'll snatch the opportunity,
And hurl her to destruction.

VARDANES.

Dread *Thermusa,*
Say, what has rous'd this tumult in thy soul?
Why dost thou rage with unabating fury,
Wild as the winds, loud as the troubl'd sea?

QUEEN.

Yes, I will tell thee — *Evanthe* — curse her —
With charms — Would that my curses had the pow'r
To kill, destroy, and blast where e'er I hate,
Then would I curse, still curse, till death should seize
The dying accents on my falt'ring tongue,
So should this world, and the false changeling man
Be buried in one universal ruin.

VARDANES.

Still err'st thou from the purpose.

QUEEN.

Ha! 'tis so —
Yes I will tell thee — for I know fond fool,
Deluded wretch, thou dotest on *Evanthe* —
Be that thy greatest curse, be curs'd like me,
With jealousy and rage, for know, the King,
Thy father, is thy rival.

SCENE IV.

VARDANES, alone.

Ha! my rival!
How knew she that? — yet stay — she's gone — my rival,
What then? he is *Arsaces'* rival too.
Ha! — this may aid and ripen my designs —
Could I but fire the King with jealousy,
And then accuse my Brother of Intrigues
Against the state — ha! — join'd with *Bethas*, and
Confed'rate with th' Arabians — 'tis most likely

That jealousy would urge him to belief.
I'll sink my claim until some fitter time,
'Til opportunity smiles on my purpose.
Lysias already has receiv'd the mandate
For *Bethas'* freedom: Let them still proceed,
This harmony shall change to discord soon.
Fortune methinks of late grows wond'rous kind,
She scarcely leaves me to employ myself.

SCENE V.

KING, ARSACES, VARDANES.

KING.

But where's *Evanthe?* Where's the lovely Maid?

ARSACES.

On the cold pavement, by her aged Sire,
The dear companion of his solitude,
She sits, nor can persuasion make her rise;
But in the wild extravagance of joy
She weeps, then smiles, like April's sun, thro' show'rs.
While with strain'd eyes he gazes on her face,
And cries, in ecstacy, "Ye gracious pow'rs!
"It is too much, it is too much to bear!"
Then clasps her to his breast, while down his cheeks
Large drops each other trace, and mix with hers.

KING.

Thy tale is moving, for my eyes o'erflow —
How slow does *Lysias* with *Evanthe* creep!
So moves old time when bringing us to bliss.

Now war shall cease, no more of war I'll have,
Death knows satiety, and pale destruction
Turns loathing from his food, thus forc'd on him.
The triffling dust, the cause of all this ruin,
The trade of death shall urge no more. —

SCENE VI.

KING, ARSACES, VARDANES, EVANTHE, LYSIAS.

KING.

Evanthe! —
See pleasure's goddess deigns to dignify
The happy scene, and make our bliss complete,
So *Venus*, from her heav'nly feat, descends
To bless the gay *Cythera* with her presence;
A thousand smiling graces wait the goddess,
A thousand little loves are flutt'ring round,
And joy is mingl'd with the beauteous train.

EVANTHE.

O! Royal Sir, thus lowly to the ground
I bend, in humble gratitude, accept
My thanks, for this thy goodness, words are vile
T' express the image of my lively thought,
And speak the grateful fulness of my heart.
All I can say, is that I now am happy,
And that thy giving hand has made me blest.

KING.

O! rise, *Evanthe* rise, this lowly posture
Suits not with charms like thine, they should command,

And ev'ry heart exult in thy behests; —
But, where's thy aged Sire?

EVANTHE.

This sudden turn
Of fortune has so wrought upon his frame,
His limbs could not support him to thy presence.

ARSACES.

This, this is truly great, this is the Hero,
Like heav'n, to scatter blessings 'mong mankind,
And e'er delight in making others happy.
Cold is the praise which waits the victor's triumph,
(Who thro' a sea has rush'd to glory),
To the o'erflowings of a grateful heart,
By obligations conquer'd: Yet, extend
Thy bounty unto me. (Kneels)

KING.

Ha! rise *Arsaces.*

ARSACES.

Not till you grant my boon.

KING.

Speak, and 'tis thine —
Wide thro' our kingdom let thy eager wishes
Search for some jewel worthy of thy seeing;
Something that's fit to show the donor's bounty,
And by the glorious sun, our worship'd God,
Thou shalt not have denial; e'en my crown
Shall gild thy brows with shining beams of Empire.
With pleasure I'll resign to thee my honours,
I long for calm retirement's softer joys.

ARSACES.

Long may you wear it, grant it bounteous heav'n,
And happiness attend it; 'tis my pray'r
That daily rises with the early sweets
Of nature's incense, and the lark's loud strain.
'Tis not the unruly transport of ambition
That urges my desires to ask your crown;
Let the vain wretch, who prides in gay dominion,
Who thinks not of the great ones weighty cares,
Enjoy his lofty wish, wide spreading rule.
The treasure which I ask, put in the scale,
Would over-balance all that Kings can boast,
Empire and diadems.

KING.

Away, that thought —
Name it, haste — speak.

ARSACES.

For all the dang'rous toil,
Thirst, hunger, marches long that I've endur'd,
For all the blood I've in thy service spent,
Reward me with *Evanthe.*

KING.

Ha! what said'st thou? —

VARDANES.

The King is mov'd, and angry bites his lip. —
Thro' my benighted soul all-chearing hope (Aside)
Beams, like an orient sun, reviving joy.

ARSACES.

The stern *Vonones* ne'er could boast a merit
But loving her.

KING.

Ah! curse the hated name —
Yes, I remember when the fell ruffian
Directed all his fury at my life;
Then sent, by pitying heav'n, t' assert the right
Of injur'd Majesty, thou, *Arsaces*,
Taught him the duty he ne'er knew before,
And laid the Traitor dead.

ARSACES.

My Royal Sire!

LYSIAS.

My Liege, the Prince still kneels.

KING.

Ha! — rebel, off — (Strikes him)
What, Lysias, did I strike thee? forgive my rage —
The name of curs'd *Vonones* fires my blood,
And gives me up to wrath. —

LYSIAS.

I am your slave,
Sway'd by your pleasure — when I forget it,
May this keen dagger, which I mean to hide,
Deep in his bosom, pierce my vitals thro'. (Aside)

KING.

Did'st thou not name *Evanthe*?

ARSACES.

I did, my Lord!
And, say, whom should I name but her, in whom
My soul has center'd all her happiness?
Nor can'st thou blame me, view her wond'rous charms,
She's all perfection; bounteous heav'n has form'd her
To be the joy, and wonder of mankind;
But language is too vile to speak her beauties.
Her ev'ry pow'r of glowing fancy's lost:
Rose blush secure, ye lilies still enjoy
Your silver whiteness, I'll not rob your charms
To deck the bright comparison; for here
It sure must fail.

KING.

He's wanton in her praise — (Aside)
I tell thee, Prince, hadst thou as many tongues,
As days have wasted since creation's birth,
They were too few to tell the mighty theme.

EVANTHE.

I'm lost! I'm lost! (Aside)

ARSACES.

Then I'll be dumb for ever.

KING.

O rash and fatal oath! is there no way,
No winding path to shun this precipice,
But must I fall and dash my hopes to atoms?
In vain I strive, thought but perplexes me,
Yet shews no hold to bear me up — now, hold
My heart a while — she's thine — 'tis done.

ARSACES.

In deep
Prostration, I thank my Royal Father.

KING.

A sudden pain shoots thro' my trembling breast —
Lend me thy arm *Vardanes* — cruel pow'rs !

SCENE VII.

ARSACES and EVANTHE.

EVANTHE. (after a pause)

E'er since the dawn of my unhappy life
Joy never shone serenely on my soul;
Still something interven'd to cloud my day.
Tell me, ye pow'rs, unfold the hidden crime
For which I'm doom'd to this eternal woe,
Thus still to number o'er my hours with tears?
The Gods are just I know, nor are decrees
In hurry shuffl'd out, but where the bolt
Takes its direction justice points the mark.
Yet still in vain I search within my breast,
I find no sins are there to shudder at —
Nought but the common frailties of our natures.
Arsaces, — Oh ! —

ARSACES.

Ha ! why that look of anguish?
Why didst thou name me with that sound of sorrow?
Ah ! say, why stream those gushing tears so fast
From their bright fountain? sparkling joy should now

Be lighten'd in thine eye, and pleasure glow
Upon thy rosy cheek; — ye sorrows hence —
'Tis love shall triumph now.

EVANTHE.

Oh! (Sighs)

ARSACES.

What means that sigh?
Tell me why heaves thy breast with such emotion?
Some dreadful thought is lab'ring for a vent,
Haste, give it loose, 'ere strengthen'd by confinement
It wrecks thy frame, and tears its snowy prison.
Is sorrow then so pleasing that you hoard it
With as much love, as misers do their gold?
Give me my share of sorrows.

EVANTHE.

Ah! too soon
You'll know what I would hide.

ARSACES.

Be it from thee —
The dreadful tale, when told by thee, shall please;
Haste, to produce it with its native terrors,
My steady soul shall still remain unshaken;
For who when bless'd with beauties like to thine
Would e'er permit a sorrow to intrude?
Far hence in darksome shades does sorrow dwell,
Where hapless wretches thro' the awful gloom,
Echo their woes, and sighing to the winds,
Augment with tears the gently murm'ring stream;
But ne'er disturbs such happiness as mine.

EVANTHE.

Oh ! 'tis not all thy boasted happiness,
Can save thee from disquietude and care;
Then build not too securely on these joys,
For envious sorrow soon will undermine,
And let the goodly structure fall to ruin.

ARSACES.

I charge thee, by our mutual vows, *Evanthe*,
Tell me, nor longer keep me in suspense:
Give me to know the utmost rage of fate.

EVANTHE.

Then know — impossible ! —

ARSACES.

Ha ! dost thou fear
To shock me? —

EVANTHE.

Know, thy Father — loves *Evanthe.* —

ARSACES.

Loves thee?

EVANTHE.

Yea, e'en to distraction loves me.
Oft at my feet he's told the moving tale,
And woo'd me with the ardency of youth.
I pitied him indeed, but that was all,
Thou would'st have pitied too.

ARSACES.

I fear 'tis true;
A thousand crouding circumstances speak it.

Ye cruel Gods! I've wreck'd a Father's peace,
Oh! bitter thought!

EVANTHE.

Didst thou observe, *Arsaces*,
How reluctant he gave me to thy arms?

ARSACES.

Yes, I observ'd that when he gave thee up,
It seem'd as tho' he gave his precious life.
And who'd forego the heav'n of thy love?
To rest on thy soft swelling breast, and in
Sweet slumbers sooth each sharp intruding care?
Oh! it were bliss, such as immortals taste,
To press thy ruby lips distilling sweets,
Or circl'd in thy snowy arms to snatch
A joy, that Gods —

EVANTHE.

Come, then, my much-lov'd Prince,
Let's seek the shelter of some kind retreat.
Happy Arabia opens wide her arms,
There may we find some friendly solitude,
Far from the noise and hurry of the Court.
Ambitious views shall never blast our joys,
Or tyrant Fathers triumph o'er our wills:
There may we live like the first happy pair
Cloath'd in primeval innocence secure.
Our food untainted by luxurious arts,
Plain, simple, as our lives, shall not destroy
The health it should sustain; while the clear brook
Affords the cooling draught our thirsts to quench.
There, hand in hand, we'll trace the citron grove,

While with the songsters' round I join my voice,
To hush thy cares and calm thy ruffl'd soul:
Or, on some flow'ry bank reclin'd, my strains
Shall captivate the natives of the stream,
While on its crystal lap ourselves we view.

ARSACES.

I see before us a wide sea of sorrows,
Th' angry waves roll forward to o'erwhelm us,
Black clouds arise, and the wind whistles loud.
But yet, oh! could I save thee from the wreck,
Thou beauteous casket, where my joys are stor'd,
Let the storm rage with double violence,
Smiling I'd view its wide extended horrors.

EVANTHE.

'Tis not enough that we do know the ill,
Say, shall we calmly see the tempest rise,
And seek no shelter from th' inclement sky,
But bid it rage? —

ARSACES.

Ha! will he force thee from me?
What, tear thee from my fond and bleeding heart?
And must I lose thee ever? dreadful word!
Never to gaze upon thy beauties more?
Never to taste the sweetness of thy lips?
Never to know the joys of mutual love?
Never! — Oh! let me lose the pow'r of thinking,
For thought is near allied to desperation.
Why, cruel Sire — why did you give me life,
And load it with a weight of wretchedness?
Take back my being, or relieve my sorrows —

Ha ! art thou not *Evanthe?* — Art thou not
Thy lovely Maid, who bless'd the fond *Arsaces.*
(Raving)

EVANTHE.

O, my lov'd Lord, recall your scatter'd spir'ts,
Alas ! I fear your senses are unsettl'd.

ARSACES.

Yes, I would leave this dull and heavy sense.
Let me grow mad; perhaps, I then may gain
Some joy, by kind imagination form'd,
Beyond reality. — O ! my *Evanthe !*
Why was I curs'd with empire? born to rule? —
Would I had been some humble Peasant's son,
And thou some Shepherd's daughter on the plain;
My throne some hillock, and my flock my subjects,
My crook my sceptre, and my faithful dog
My only guard; nor curs'd with dreams of greatness.
At early dawn I'd hail the coming day,
And join the lark the rival of his lay;
At sultry noon to some kind shade repair,
Thus joyful pass the hours, my only care,
To guard my flock, and please the yielding Fair.

SCENE VIII.

KING. — VARDANES, behind the *Scene.*

KING.

I will not think, to think is torment — Ha !
See, how they twine ! ye furies cut their hold.

Now their hot blood beats loud to love's alarms;
Sigh presses sigh, while from their sparkling eyes
Flashes desire — Oh ! ye bright heav'nly beings,
Who pitying bend to suppliant Lovers pray'rs,
And aid them in extremity, assist me !

VARDANES.

Thus, for the Trojan, mourn'd the Queen of Carthage;
So, on the shore she raving stood, and saw
His navy leave her hospitable shore.
In vain she curs'd the wind which fill'd their sails,
And bore the emblem of its change away.
(Comes forward)

KING.

Vardanes — ha ! — come here, I know thou lov'st me.

VARDANES.

I do my Lord, but, say, what busy villain
Durst e'er approach your ear, with coz'ning tales,
And urge you to a doubt?

KING.

None, none believe me.
I'll ne'er oppress thy love with fearful doubt —
A little nigher — let me lean upon thee —
And thou be my support — for now I mean
T' unbosom to thee free without restraint:
Search all the deep recesses of my soul,
And open ev'ry darling thought before thee,
Which long I've secreted with jealous care.
Pray, mark me well.

VARDANES.

I will, my Royal Sire.

KING.

On *Anna* thus reclin'd the love-sick Dido;
Thus to her cheek laid hers with gentle pressure,
And wet her sister with a pearly show'r,
Which fell from her sad eyes, then told her tale,
While gentle *Anna* gave a pitying tear,
And own'd 'twas moving — thou canst pity too,
I know thy nature tender and engaging.

VARDANES.

Tell me, my gracious Lord, what moves you thus?
Why is your breast distracted with these tumults?
Teach me some method how to sooth your sorrows,
And give your heart its former peace and joy;
Instruct, thy lov'd, *Vardanes.* —

KING.

Yes, I'll tell thee;
But listen with attention while I speak;
And yet I know 'twill shock thy gentle soul,
And horror o'er thee 'll spread his palsy hand.
O, my lov'd Son! thou fondness of my age!
Thou art the prop of my declining years,
In thee alone I find a Father's joy,
Of all my offspring: But *Arsaces* —

VARDANES.

Ha!
My Brother! —

KING.

Ay — why dost start? — thy Brother
Pursues me with his hate: and, while warm life
Rolls the red current thro' my veins, delights

To see me tortur'd; with an easy smile
He meets my suff'rings, and derides my pain.

VARDANES.

Oh!

KING.

What means that hollow groan? — *Vardanes,* speak,
Death's image sits upon thy pallid cheek,
While thy low voice sounds as when murmurs run
Thro' lengthen'd vaults —

VARDANES.

O! my foreboding thoughts, (Aside)
'Twas this disturb'd my rest; when sleep at night
Lock'd me in slumbers; in my dreams I saw
My Brother's crime — yet death! — it cannot be —

KING.

Ha! — What was that? —

VARDANES.

O! my dread Lord, some Villain
Bred up in lies, and train'd to treach'ry,
Has injur'd you by vile reports, to stain
My Princely Brother's honour.

KING.

Thou know'st more,
Thy looks confess what thou in vain wouldst hide —
And hast thou then conspir'd against me too,
And sworn concealment to your practices? —
Thy guilt —

VARDANES.

Ha! guilt! — what guilt? —

KING.

Nay, start not so —
I'll know your purposes, spite of thy art.

VARDANES.

O! ye great Gods! and is it come to this? —
My Royal Father call your reason home,
Drive these loud passions hence, that thus deform you.
My Brother — Ah! what shall I say? — My Brother
Sure loves you as he ought.

KING.

Ha! as he ought? —
Hell blister thy evasive tongue — I'll know it —
I will; I'll search thy breast, thus will I open
A passage to your secrets — yet resolv'd —
Yet steady in your horrid villany —
'Tis fit that I from whom such monsters sprung
No more should burthen earth — Ye Parricides! —
Here plant your daggers in this hated bosom —
Here rive my heart, and end at once my sorrows,
I gave ye being, that's the mighty crime.

VARDANES.

I can no more — here let me bow in anguish —
Think not that I e'er join'd in his designs,
Because I have conceal'd my knowledge of them;
I meant, by pow'rful reason's friendly aid,
To turn him from destruction's dreadful path.
And bring him to a sense of what he ow'd
To you as King and Father.

KING.

Say on — I'll hear.

VARDANES.

He views thy sacred life with envious hate,
And 'tis a bar to his ambitious hopes.
On the bright throne of Empire his plum'd wishes
Seat him, while on his proud aspiring brows
He feels the pleasing weight of Royalty.
But when he wakes from these his airy dreams,
(Delusions form'd by the deceiver hope,
To raise him to the glorious height of greatness)
Then hurl him from proud Empire to subjection.
Wild wrath will quickly swell his haughty breast,
Soon as he finds 'tis but a shadowy blessing. —
'Twas fav'ring accident discover'd to me
All that I know; this Evening as I stood
Alone, retir'd, in the still gallery,
That leads up to th' appartment of my Brother,
T' indulge my melancholy thoughts, —

KING.

Proceed —

VARDANES.

A wretch approach'd with wary step, his eye
Spoke half his tale, denoting villany.
In hollow murmurs thus he question'd me.
Was I the Prince? — I answer'd to content him —
Then in his hand he held this paper forth.
"Take this, says he, this *Bethas* greets thee with,
"Keep but your word our plot will meet success."
I snatch'd it with more rashness than discretion,
Which taught him his mistake. In haste he drew,

And aim'd his dagger at my breast, but paid
His life, a forfeit, for his bold presuming.

KING.

O Villain! Villain!

VARDANES.

Here, read this, my lord —
I read it, and cold horror froze my blood,
And shook me like an ague.

KING.

Ha! — what's this? —
"Doubt not Arabia's aid, set me but free,
"I'll easy pass on the old cred'lous King,
"For fair *Evanthe's* Father." — Thus to atoms —
Oh! could I tear these cursed traitors thus.
(tears the paper into pieces)

VARDANES.

Curses avail you nothing, he has pow'r,
And may abuse it to your prejudice.

KING.

I am resolv'd —

VARDANES.

Tho' Pris'ner in his camp,
Yet, *Bethas* was attended like a Prince,
As tho' he still commanded the Arabians.
'Tis true, when they approach'd the royal city,
He threw him into chains to blind our eyes,
A shallow artifice —

KING.

That is a Truth.

VARDANES.

And, yet, he is your Son.

KING.

Ah ! that indeed —

VARDANES.

Why that still heightens his impiety,
To rush to empire thro' his Father's blood,
And, in return of life, to give him death.

KING.

Oh ! I am all on fire, yes I must tear
These folds of venom from me.

VARDANES.

Sure 'twas *Lysias*
That cross'd the passage now.

KING.

'Tis to my wish.
I'll in, and give him orders to arrest
My traitor Son and *Bethas* — Now *Vardanes*
Indulge thy Father in this one request —
Seize, with some horse, *Evanthe*, and bear her
To your command — Oh ! I'll own my weakness —
I love with fondness mortal never knew —
Nor Jove himself, when he forsook his heav'n,
And in a brutal shape disgrac'd the God,
E'er lov'd like me.

VARDANES.

I will obey you, Sir.

SCENE IX.

VARDANES, alone.

I'll seize her, but I'll keep her for myself,
It were a sin to give her to his age —
To twine the blooming garland of the spring
Around the sapless trunks of wither'd oaks —
The night, methinks, grows ruder than it was,
Thus should it be, thus nature should be shock'd,
And Prodigies, affrighting all mankind,
Foretell the dreadful business I intend.
The earth should gape, and swallow cities up,
Shake from their haughty heights aspiring tow'rs,
And level mountains with the vales below;
The Sun amaz'd should frown in dark eclipse,
And light retire to its unclouded heav'n;
While darkness, bursting from her deep recess,
Should wrap all nature in eternal night. —
Ambition, glorious fever of the mind,
'Tis that which raises us above mankind;
The shining mark which bounteous heav'n has gave,
From vulgar souls distinguishing the brave.

END of the THIRD *ACT*.

ACT IV. — SCENE I.

A PRISON.

GOTARZES and PHRAATES.

PHRAATES.

Oh! fly my Prince, for safety dwells not here,
Hence let me urge thy flight with eager haste.
Last night thy Father sigh'd his soul to bliss,
Base murther'd —

GOTARZES.

Murther'd? ye Gods! —

PHRAATES.

Alas! 'tis true.
Stabb'd in his slumber by a traitor's hand;
I scarce can speak it — horror choaks my words —
Lysias it was who did the damned deed,
Urg'd by the bloody Queen, and his curs'd rage,
Because the King, thy Sire, in angry mood,
Once struck him on his foul dishonest cheek.
Suspicion gave me fears of this, when first
I heard, the Prince, *Arsaces*, was imprison'd,
By fell *Vardanes'* wiles.

GOTARZES.

Oh! horror! horror!
Hither I came to share my Brother's sorrows,

To mingle tears, and give him sigh for sigh;
But this is double, double weight of woe.

PHRAATES.

'Tis held as yet a secret from the world.
Frighted by hideous dreams I shook off sleep,
And as I mus'd the garden walks along,
Thro' the deep gloom, close in a neighb'ring walk,
Vardanes with proud *Lysias* I beheld,
Still eager in discourse they saw not me,
For yet the early dawn had not appear'd;
I sought a secret stand, where hid from view,
I heard stern *Lysias*, hail the Prince *Vardanes*
As Parthia's dreaded Lord — "'Tis done, he cry'd,
"'Tis done, and *Artabanus* is no more.
"The blow he gave me is repay'd in blood;
"Now shall the morn behold two rising suns:
"*Vardanes* thou, our better light, shalt bring
"Bright day and joy to ev'ry heart."

GOTARZES.

Why slept
Your vengeance, oh! ye righteous Gods?

PHRAATES.

Then told
A tale, so fill'd with bloody circumstance,
Of this damn'd deed, that stiffen'd me with horror.
Vardanes seem'd to blame the hasty act,
As rash, and unadvis'd, by the passion urg'd,
Which never yields to cool reflection's place.
But, being done, resolv'd it secret, least
The multitude should take it in their wise

Authority to pry into his death.
Arsaces was, by assassination,
Doom'd to fall. Your name was mention'd also —
But hurried by my fears away, I left
The rest unheard —

GOTARZES.

What can be done? — Reflection, why wilt thou
Forsake us, when distress is at our heels?
Phraates help me, aid me with thy council.

PHRAATES.

Then stay not here, fly to *Barzaphernes*,
His conqu'ring troops are at a trivial distance;
Soon will you reach the camp; he lov'd your Brother,
And your Father with affection serv'd; haste
Your flight, whilst yet I have the city-guard,
For *Lysias* I expect takes my command,
I to the camp dispatch'd a trusty slave,
Before the morn had spread her blushing veil,
Away, you'll meet the Gen'ral on the road.
On such a cause as this he'll not delay.

GOTARZES.

I thank your love —

SCENE II.

PHRAATES, alone.

I'll wait behind, my stay
May aid the cause; dissembling I must learn,
Necessity shall teach me how to vary

My features to the looks of him I serve.
I'll thrust myself disguis'd among the croud,
And fill their ears with murmurs of the deed:
Whisper all is not well, blow up the sparks
Of discord, and it soon will flame to rage.

SCENE III.

QUEEN and LYSIAS.

QUEEN.

Haste, and shew me to the Prince *Arsaces*,
Delay not, see the signet of *Vardanes*.

LYSIAS.

Royal *Thermusa*, why this eagerness?
This tumult of the soul? — what means this dagger?
Ha! — I suspect —

QUEEN.

Hold — for I'll tell thee, *Lysias*.
'Tis — oh! I scarce can speak the mighty joy —
I shall be greatly blest in dear revenge,
'Tis vengeance on *Arsaces* — yes, this hand
Shall urge the shining poniard to his heart,
And give him death — yea, give the ruffian death;
So shall I smile on his keen agonies.

LYSIAS.

Ha! am I robb'd of all my hopes of vengeance,
Shall I then calmly stand with all my wrongs,
And see another bear away revenge?

QUEEN.

For what can *Lysias* ask revenge, to bar
His Queen of hers?

LYSIAS.

Was I not scorn'd, and spurn'd,
With haughty insolence? like a base coward
Refus'd what e'er I ask'd, and call'd a boaster?
My honour sullied, with opprobrious words,
Which can no more its former brightness know,
'Til, with his blood, I've wash'd the stains away.
Say, shall I then not seek for glorious vengeance?

QUEEN.

And what is this, to the sad Mother's griefs,
Her hope cut off, rais'd up with pain and care?
Hadst thou e'er supported the lov'd Prattler?
Hadst thou like me hung o'er his infancy,
Wasting in wakeful mood the tedious night,
And watch'd his sickly couch, far mov'd from rest,
Waiting his health's return? — Ah! hadst thou known
The parent's fondness, rapture, toil and sorrow,
The joy his actions gave, and the fond wish
Of something yet to come, to bless my age,
And lead me down with pleasure to the grave,
Thou wouldst not thus talk lightly of my wrongs.
But I delay —

LYSIAS.

To thee I then submit.
Be sure to wreak a double vengeance on him;
If that thou knowst a part in all his body,
Where pain can most be felt, strike, strike him there —

And let him know the utmost height of anguish.
It is a joy to think that he shall fall,
Tho' 'tis another hand which gives the blow.

SCENE IV.

ARSACES and BETHAS.

ARSACES.

Why should I linger out my joyless days,
When length of hope is length of misery?
Hope is a coz'ner, and beguiles our cares,
Cheats us with empty shews of happiness,
Swift fleeting joys which mock the faint embrace;
We wade thro' ills pursuing of the meteor,
Yet are distanc'd still.

BETHAS.

Ah! talk not of hope —
Hope fled when bright *Astræa* spurn'd this earth,
And sought her seat among the shining Gods;
Despair, proud tyrant, ravages my breast,
And makes all desolation.

ARSACES.

How can I
Behold those rev'rent sorrows, see those cheeks
Moist with the dew which falls from thy sad eyes,
Nor imitate distraction's frantic tricks,
And chace cold lifeless reason from her throne?
I am the fatal cause of all this sorrow,
The spring of ills, — to know me is unhappiness; —

And mis'ry, like a hateful plague, pursues
My wearied steps, and blasts the springing verdure.

BETHAS.

No; — It is I that am the source of all,
It is my fortune sinks you to this trouble;
Before you shower'd your gentle pity on me,
You shone the pride of this admiring world. —
Evanthe springs from me, whose fatal charms
Produces all this ruin — Hear me heav'n !
If to another love she ever yields,
And stains her soul with spotted falsehood's crime,
If e'en in expectation tastes a bliss,
Nor joins *Arsaces* with it, I will wreck
My vengeance on her, so that she shall be
A dread example to all future times.

ARSACES.

Oh ! curse her not, nor threaten her with anger,
She is all gentleness, yet firm to truth,
And blest with ev'ry pleasing virtue, free
From levity, her sexes character.
She scorns to chace the turning of the wind,
Varying from point to point.

BETHAS.

I love her, ye Gods !
I need not speak the greatness of my love,
Each look which straining draws my soul to hers
Denotes unmeasur'd fondness; but mis'ry,
Like a fretful peevish child, can scarce tell
What it would wish, or aim at.

ARSACES.

Immortals, hear!
Thus do I bow my soul in humble pray'r —
Thou, King of beings, in whose breath is fate,
Show'r on *Evanthe* all thy choicest blessings,
And bless her with excess of happiness;
If yet, there is one bliss reserv'd in store,
And written to my name, oh! give it her,
And give me all her sorrows in return.

BETHAS.

'Rise, 'rise my Prince, this goodness o'erwhelms me,
She's too unworthy of so great a passion.

ARSACES.

I know not what it means, I'm not as usual,
Ill-boding cares, and restless fears oppress me,
And horrid dreams disturb, and fright, my slumbers;
But yesternight, 'tis dreadful to relate,
E'en now I tremble at my waking thoughts,
Methought, I stood alone upon the shore,
And, at my feet, there roll'd a sea of blood,
High wrought, and 'midst the waves, appear'd my Father
Struggling for life; above him was *Vardanes*,
Pois'd in the air, he seem'd to rule the storm,
And, now and then, would push my Father down,
And for a space he'd sink beneath the waves,
And then, all gory, rise to open view,
His voice in broken accents reach'd my ear,
And bade me save him from the bloody stream;
Thro' the red billows eagerly I rush'd,
But sudden woke, benum'd with chilling fear.

BETHAS.

Most horrible indeed! — but let it pass,
'Tis but the offspring of a mind disturb'd,
For sorrow leaves impressions on the fancy,
Which shew most fearful to us lock'd in sleep.

ARSACES.

Thermusa! ha! — what can be her design?
She bears this way, and carries in her looks
An eagerness importing violence.
Retire — for I would meet her rage alone.

SCENE V.

ARSACES and QUEEN.

ARSACES.

What means the proud *Thermusa* by this visit,
Stoops heav'n-born pity to a breast like thine?
Pity adorns th' virtuous, but ne'er dwells
Where hate, revenge, and rage distract the soul.
Sure, it is hate that hither urg'd thy steps,
To view misfortune with an eye of triumph.
I know thou lov'st me not, for I have dar'd
To cross thy purposes, and, bold in censure,
Spoke of thy actions as they merited.
Besides, this hand 'twas slew the curs'd *Vonones.*

QUEEN.

And darst thou insolent to name *Vonones?*
To heap perdition on thy guilty soul?

There needs not this to urge me to revenge —
But let me view this wonder of mankind,
Whose breath can set the bustling world in arms.
I see no dreadful terrors in his eye,
Nor gathers chilly fears around my heart,
Nor strains my gazing eye with admiration,
And, tho' a woman, I can strike the blow.

ARSACES.

Why gaze you on me thus? why hesitate?
Am I to die?

QUEEN.

Thou art — this dagger shall
Dissolve thy life, thy fleeting ghost I'll send
To wait *Vonones* in the shades below.

ARSACES.

And even there I'll triumph over him.

QUEEN.

O, thou vile homicide! thy fatal hand
Has robb'd me of all joy; *Vonones*, to
Thy *Manes* this proud sacrifice I give.
That hand which sever'd the friendship of thy
Soul and body, shall never draw again
Imbitt'ring tears from sorr'wing mother's eyes.
This, with the many tears I've shed, receive —
(Offers to stab him)
Ha! — I'd strike; what holds my hand? — 'tis n't pity.

ARSACES.

Nay, do not mock me, with the shew of death,
And yet deny the blessing; I have met

Your taunts with equal taunts, in hopes to urge
The blow with swift revenge; but since that fails,
I'll woo thee to compliance, teach my tongue
Persuasion's winning arts, to gain thy soul;
I'll praise thy clemency, in dying accents
Bless thee for, this, thy charitable deed,
Oh! do not stand; see, how my bosom heaves
To meet the stroke; in pity let me die,
'Tis all the happiness I now can know.

QUEEN.

How sweet the eloquence of dying men!
Hence Poets feign'd the music of the Swan,
When death upon her lays his icy hand,
She melts away in melancholy strains.

ARSACES.

Play not thus cruel with my poor request,
But take my loving Father's thanks, and mine.

QUEEN.

Thy Father cannot thank me now.

ARSACES.

He will,
Believe me, e'en whilst dissolv'd in ecstacy
On fond *Evanthe's* bosom, he will pause,
One moment from his joys, to bless the deed.

QUEEN.

What means this tumult in my breast? from whence
Proceeds this sudden change? my heart beats high,

And soft compassion makes me less than woman:
I'll search no more for what I fear to know.

ARSACES.

Why drops the dagger from thy trembling hand?
O! yet be kind —

QUEEN.

No: now I'd have thee live,
Since it is happiness to die: 'Tis pain
That I would give thee, thus I bid thee live;
Yes, I would have thee a whole age a dying,
And smile to see thy ling'ring agonies.
All day I'd watch thee, mark each heighten'd pang,
While springing joy should swell my panting bosom;
This I would have — But should this dagger give
Thy soul the liberty it fondly wishes,
'Twould soar aloft, and mock my faint revenge.

ARSACES.

This mildness shews most foul, thy anger lovely.
Think that 'twas I who blasted thy fond hope,
Vonones now lies number'd with the dead,
And all your joys are buried in his grave;
My hand untimely pluck'd the precious flow'r,
Before its shining beauties were display'd.

QUEEN.

O Woman! Woman! where's thy resolution?
Where's thy revenge? Where's all thy hopes of vengeance?
Giv'n to the winds — Ha! is it pity? — No —
I fear it wears another softer name.

I'll think no more, but rush to my revenge,
In spite of foolish fear, or woman's softness;
Be steady now my soul to thy resolves.
Yes, thou shalt die, thus, on thy breast, I write
Thy instant doom — Ha! — ye Gods!

(QUEEN starts, as, in great fright, at hearing something)

ARSACES.

Why this pause?
Why dost thou idly stand like imag'd vengeance,
With harmless terrors threatning on thy brow,
With lifted arm, yet canst not strike the blow?

QUEEN.

It surely was the Echo to my fears,
The whistling wind, perhaps, which mimick'd voice;
But thrice methought it loudly cry'd, "forbear."
Imagination hence — I'll heed thee not —

(Ghost of ARTABANUS rises)

Save me — oh! — save me — ye eternal pow'rs! —
See! — see it comes, surrounded with dread terrors —
Hence — hence! nor blast me with that horrid sight —
Throw off that shape, and search th' infernal rounds
For horrid forms, there's none can shock like thine.

GHOST.

No; I will ever wear this form, thus e'er
Appear before thee; glare upon thee thus,
'Til desperation, join'd to thy damn'd crime,
Shall wind thee to the unmost height of frenzy,
In vain you grasp the dagger in your hand,

In vain you dress your brows in angry frowns,
In vain you raise your threatning arm in air,
Secure, *Arsaces* triumphs o'er your rage.
Guarded by fate, from thy accurs'd revenge,
Thou canst not touch his life; the Gods have giv'n
A softness to thy more than savage soul
Before unknown, to aid their grand designs.
Fate yet is lab'ring with some great event,
But what must follow I'm forbid to broach —
Think, think of me, I sink to rise again,
To play in blood before thy aking sight,
And shock thy guilty soul with hell-born horrors —
Think, think of *Artabanus!* and despair — (Sinks)

QUEEN.

Think of thee, and despair? — yes, I'll despair —
Yet stay, — oh! stay, thou messenger of fate!
Tell me — Ha! 'tis gone — and left me wretched —

ARSACES.

Your eyes seem fix'd upon some dreadful object,
Horror and anguish cloath your whiten'd face,
And your frame shakes with terror; I hear you speak
As seeming earnest in discourse, yet hear
No second voice.

QUEEN.

What! saw'st thou nothing?

ARSACES.

Nothing.

QUEEN.

Nor hear'd? —

ARSACES.

Nor hear'd.

QUEEN.

Amazing spectacle! —
Cold moist'ning dews distil from ev'ry pore,
I tremble like to palsied age — Ye Gods!
Would I could leave this loath'd detested being! —
Oh! all my brain's on fire — I rave! I rave! —
(Ghost rises again)
Ha! it comes again — see, it glides along —
See, see, what streams of blood flow from its wounds!
A crimson torrent — Shield me, oh! shield me, heav'n. —

ARSACES.

Great, and righteous Gods! —

QUEEN.

Ah! frown not on me —
Why dost thou shake thy horrid locks at me?
Can I give immortality? — 'tis gone — (Ghost sinks)
It flies me, see, ah! — stop it, stop it, haste —

ARSACES.

Oh, piteous sight! —

QUEEN.

Hist! prithee hist! — oh death!
I'm all on fire — now freezing bolts of ice
Dart thro' my breast — Oh! burst ye cords of life —
Ha! who are ye? — Why do ye stare upon me? —
Oh! — defend me, from these bick'ring Furies!

ARSACES.

Alas! her sense is lost, distressful Queen!

QUEEN.

Help me, thou King of Gods! oh! help me! help! —
See! they envir'n me round — *Vonones* too,
The foremost leading on the dreadful troop —
But there, *Vardanes* beck'ns me to shun
Their hellish rage — I come, I come!
Ah! they pursue me, with a scourge of fire. —
(Runs out distracted)

SCENE VI.

ARSACES, alone.

Oh! — horror! — on the ground she breathless lies,
Silent, in death's cold sleep; the wall besmear'd
With brains and gore the marks of her despair.
O guilt! how dreadful dost thou ever shew!
How lovely are the charms of innocence!
How beauteous tho' in sorrows and distress! —
Ha! — what noise? — (Clashing of swords)

SCENE VII.

ARSACES, BARZAPHERNES and GOTARZES.

BARZAPHERNES.

At length we've forc'd our entrance —
O my lov'd Prince! to see thee thus, indeed,
Melts e'en me to a woman's softness; see
My eyes o'erflow — Are these the ornaments
For Royal hands? rude manacles! oh shameful!

Is this thy room of state, this gloomy goal?
Without attendance, and thy bed the pavement?
But, ah! how diff'rent was our parting last!
When flush'd with vict'ry, reeking from the slaughter,
You saw Arabia's Sons scour o'er the plain
In shameful flight, before your conqu'ring sword;
Then shone you like the God of battle.

ARSACES.

Welcome! —
Welcome, my loyal friends! *Barzaphernes!*
My good old soldier, to my bosom thus!
Gotarzes, my lov'd Brother! now I'm happy. —
But, say, my soldier, why these threatning arms?
Why am I thus releas'd by force? my Father,
I should have said the King, had he relented,
He'd not have us'd this method to enlarge me.
Alas! I fear, too forward in your love,
You'll brand me with the rebel's hated name.

BARZAPHERNES.

I am by nature blunt — the soldier's manner.
Unus'd to the soft arts practis'd at courts.
Nor can I move the passions, or disguise
The sorr'wing tale to mitigate the smart.
Then seek it not: I would sound the alarm,
Loud as the trumpet's clangour, in your ears;
Nor will I hail you, as our Parthia's King,
'Til you've full reveng'd your Father's murther.

ARSACES.

Murther? — good heav'n!

BARZAPHERNES.

The tale requires some time;
And opportunity must not be lost;
Your traitor Brother, who usurps your rights,
Must, 'ere his faction gathers to a head,
Have from his brows his new-born honours torn.

ARSACES.

What, dost thou say, murther'd by *Vardanes?*
Impious parricide! — detested villain! —
Give me a sword, and onward to the charge,
Stop gushing tears, for I will weep in blood,
And sorrow with the groans of dying men. —
Revenge! revenge! — oh! — all my soul's on fire!

GOTARZES.

'Twas not *Vardanes* struck the fatal blow,
Though, great in pow'r usurp'd, he dares support
The actor, vengeful *Lysias;* to his breast
He clasps, with grateful joy, the bloody villain;
Who soon meant, with ruffian wiles, to cut
You from the earth, and also me.

ARSACES.

Just heav'ns! —
But, gentle Brother, how didst thou elude
The vigilant, suspicious, tyrant's craft.

GOTARZES.

Phraates, by an accident, obtain'd
The knowledge of the deed, and warn'd by him
I bent my flight toward the camp, to seek
Protection and revenge; but scarce I'd left
The city when I o'ertook the Gen'ral.

BARZAPHERNES.

'Ere the sun 'rose I gain'd th' intelligence:
The soldiers when they heard the dreadful tale,
First stood aghast, and motionless with horror.
Then suddenly, inspir'd with noble rage,
Tore up their ensigns, calling on their leaders
To march them to the city instantly.
I, with some trusty few, with speed came forward,
To raise our friends within, and gain your freedom.
Nor hazard longer, by delays, your safety.
Already faithful *Phraates* has gain'd
A num'rous party of the citizens;
With these we mean t' attack the Royal Palace,
Crush the bold tyrant with surprize, while sunk
In false security; and vengeance wreck,
'Ere that he thinks the impious crime be known.

ARSACES.

O! parent being, Ruler of yon heav'n!
Who bade creation spring to order, hear me.
What ever sins are laid upon my soul,
Now let them not prove heavy on this day,
To sink my arm, or violate my cause.
The sacred rights of Kings, my Country's wrongs,
The punishment of fierce impiety,
And a lov'd Father's death, call forth my sword —

Now on; I feel all calm within my breast,
And ev'ry busy doubt is hush'd to rest;
Smile heav'n propitious on my virtuous cause,
Nor aid the wretch who dares disdain your laws.

END of the FOURTH *ACT*.

ACT V. — SCENE I.

THE PALACE.

The Curtain rises, slowly, to soft music, and discovers EVANTHE sleeping on a Sofa; after the music ceases, VARDANES enters.

VARDANES.

Now shining Empire standing at the goal,
Beck'ns me forward to increase my speed;
But yet, *Arsaces* lives, bane to my hopes,
Lysias I'll urge to ease me of his life,
Then give the villain up to punishment.
The shew of justice gains the changeling croud.
Besides, I ne'er will harbour in my bosom
Such serpents, ever ready with their stings —
But now one hour for love and fair *Evanthe* —
Hence with ambition's cares — see, where reclin'd,
In slumbers all her sorrows are dismiss'd,
Sleep seems to heighten ev'ry beauteous feature,
And adds peculiar softness to each grace.
She weeps — in dreams some lively sorrow pains her —
I'll take one kiss — oh ! what a balmy sweetness !
Give me another — and another still —
For ever thus I'd dwell upon her lips.
Be still my heart, and calm unruly transports. —
Wake her, with music, from this mimic death.

(Music sounds)

SONG.

Tell me, Phillis, tell me why,
  You appear so wond'rous coy,
When that glow, and sparkling eye,
  Speak you want to taste the joy?
Prithee give this fooling o'er,
Nor torment your lover more.

While youth is warm within our veins,
  And nature tempts us to be gay,
Give to pleasure loose the reins,
  Love and youth fly swift away.
Youth in pleasure should be spent,
Age will come, we'll then repent.

EVANTHE (waking)

I come ye lovely shades — Ha! am I here?
Still in the tyrant's palace? Ye bright pow'rs!
Are all my blessings then but vis'onary?
Methought I was arriv'd on that blest shore
Where happy souls for ever dwell, crown'd with
Immortal bliss; *Arsaces* led me through
The flow'ry groves, while all around me gleam'd
Thousand and thousand shades, who welcom'd me
With pleasing songs of joy — *Vardanes*, ha! —

VARDANES.

Why beams the angry lightning of thine eye
Against thy sighing slave? Is love a crime?
Oh! if to dote, with such excess of passion
As rises e'en to mad extravagance
Is criminal, I then am so, indeed.

EVANTHE.

Away! vile man! —

VARDANES.

If to pursue thee e'er
With all the humblest offices of love,
If ne'er to know one single thought that does
Not bear thy bright idea, merits scorn —

EVANTHE.

Hence from my sight — nor let me, thus, pollute
Mine eyes, with looking on a wretch like thee,
Thou cause of all my ills; I sicken at
Thy loathsome presence —

VARDANES.

'Tis not always thus,
Nor dost thou ever meet the sounds of love
With rage and fierce disdain: *Arsaces*, soon,
Could smooth thy brow, and melt thy icy breast.

EVANTHE.

Ha! does it gall thee? Yes, he could, he could;
Oh! when he speaks, such sweetness dwells upon
His accents, all my soul dissolves to love,
And warm desire; such truth and beauty join'd!
His looks are soft and kind, such gentleness!
Such virtue swells his bosom! in his eye
Sits majesty, commanding ev'ry heart.
Strait as the pine, the pride of all the grove,
More blooming than the spring, and sweeter far,
Than asphodels or roses infant sweets.
Oh! I could dwell forever on his praise,
Yet think eternity was scarce enough

To tell the mighty theme; here in my breast
His image dwells, but one dear thought of him,
When fancy paints his Person to my eye,
As he was wont in tenderness dissolv'd,
Sighing his vows, or kneeling at my feet,
Wipes off all mem'ry of my wretchedness.

VARDANES.

I know this brav'ry is affected, yet
It gives me joy, to think my rival only
Can in imagination taste thy beauties.
Let him, — 'twill ease him in his solitude,
And gild the horrors of his prison-house,
Till death shall —

EVANTHE.

Ha! what was that? till death — ye Gods!
Ah, now I feel distress's tort'ring pang —
Thou canst not villain — darst not think his death —
O mis'ry! —

VARDANES.

Naught but your kindness saves him,
Yet bless me, with your love, and he is safe;
But the same frown which kills my growing hopes,
Gives him to death.

EVANTHE.

O horror, I could die
Ten thousand times to save the lov'd *Arsaces.*
Teach me the means, ye pow'rs, how to save him:
Then lead me to what ever is my fate.

VARDANES.

Not only shall he die, but to thy view
I'll bring the scene, those eyes that take delight

In cruelty, shall have enough of death.
E'en here, before thy sight, he shall expire,
Not sudden, but by ling'ring torments; all
That mischief can invent shall be practis'd
To give him pain; to lengthen out his woe
I'll search around the realm for skillful men,
To find new tortures.

EVANTHE.

Oh! wrack not thus my soul!

VARDANES.

The sex o'erflows with various humours, he
Who catches not their smiles the very moment,
Will lose the blessing — I'll improve this softness. —
(Aside to her)
— Heav'n never made thy beauties to destroy,
They were to bless, and not to blast mankind;
Pity should dwell within thy lovely breast,
That sacred temple ne'er was form'd for hate
A habitation; but a residence
For love and gaiety.

EVANTHE.

Oh! heav'ns!

VARDANES.

That sigh,
Proclaims your kind consent to save *Arsaces.*
(Laying hold of her)

EVANTHE.

Ha! villain, off — unhand me — hence —

VARDANES.

In vain
Is opportunity to those, who spend

An idle courtship on the fair, they well
Deserve their fate, if they're disdain'd; — her charms
To rush upon, and conquer opposition,
Gains the Fair one's praise; an active lover
Suits, who lies aside the coxcomb's empty whine,
And forces her to bliss.

EVANTHE.

Ah! hear me, hear me,
Thus kneeling, with my tears, I do implore thee:
Think on my innocence, nor force a joy
Which will ever fill thy soul with anguish.
Seek not to load my ills with infamy,
Let me not be a mark for bitter scorn,
To bear proud virtue's taunts and mocking jeers,
And like a flow'r, of all its sweetness robb'd,
Be trod to earth, neglected and disdain'd,
And spurn'd by ev'ry vulgar saucy foot.

VARDANES.

Speak, speak forever — music's in thy voice,
Still attentive will I listen to thee,
Be hush'd as night, charm'd with the magic sound.

EVANTHE.

Oh! teach me, heav'n, soft moving eloquence,
To bend his stubborn soul to gentleness. —
Where is thy virtue? Where thy princely lustre?
Ah! wilt thou meanly stoop to do a wrong,
And stain thy honour with so foul a blot?
Thou who shouldst be a guard to innocence.
Leave force to brutes — for pleasure is not found

Where still the soul's averse; horror and guilt,
Distraction, desperation chace her hence.
Some happier gentle Fair one you may find,
Whose yielding heart may bend to meet your flame,
In mutual love soft joys alone are found;
When souls are drawn by secret sympathy,
And virtue does on virtue smile.

VARDANES.

No more —
Her heav'nly tongue will charm me from th' intent.—
Hence coward softness, force shall make me blest.

EVANTHE.

Assist me, ye bless't pow'rs! — oh! strike, ye Gods!
Strike me, with thunder dead, this moment, e'er
I suffer violation —

VARDANES.

'Tis in vain,
The idle pray'rs by fancy'd grief put up,
Are blown by active winds regardless by,
Nor ever reach the heav'ns.

SCENE II.

VARDANES, EVANTHE, and LYSIAS.

LYSIAS.

Arm, arm, my Lord! —

VARDANES.

Damnation! why this interruption now? —

LYSIAS.

Oh! arm! my noble Prince, the foe's upon us.
Arsaces, by *Barzaphernes* releas'd,
Join'd with the citizens, assaults the Palace,
And swears revenge for *Artabanus'* death.

VARDANES.

Ha! what? revenge for *Artabanus'* death?—
'Tis the curse of Princes that their counsels,
Which should be kept like holy mysteries,
Can never rest in silent secrecy.
Fond of employ, some cursed tattling tongue
Will still divulge them.

LYSIAS.

Sure some fiend from hell
In mischief eminent, to cross our views,
Has giv'n th' intelligence, for man could not.

EVANTHE.

Oh! ever blest event!—All-gracious heav'n!
This beam of joy revives me.

SCENE III.

VARDANES, EVANTHE, LYSIAS, to them, an OFFICER.

OFFICER.

Haste! my Lord!
Or all will soon be lost; tho' thrice repuls'd
By your e'erfaithful guards, they still return
With double fury.

VARDANES.

Hence, then, idle love —
Come forth, my trusty sword — curs'd misfortune! —
Had I but one short hour, without reluctance,
I'd meet them, tho' they brib'd the pow'rs of hell,
To place their furies in the van: Yea, rush
To meet this dreadful Brother 'midst the war —
Haste to the combat — Now a crown or death —
The wretch who dares to give an inch of ground
Till I retire, shall meet the death he shun'd.
Away — away! delays are dang'rous now —

SCENE IV.

EVANTHE, alone.

Now heav'n be partial to *Arsaces*' cause,
Nor leave to giddy chance when virtue strives;
Let victory sit on his warlike helm,
For justice draws his sword: be thou his aid,
And let the opposer's arm sink with the weight
Of his most impious crimes — be still my heart,
For all that thou canst aid him with is pray'r.
Oh! that I had the strength of thousands in me!
Or that my voice could wake the sons of men
To join, and crush the tyrant! —

SCENE V.

EVANTHE and CLEONE.

EVANTHE.

My *Cleone* —
Welcome thou partner of my joys and sorrows.

CLEONE.

Oh ! yonder terror triumphs uncontroul'd,
And glutton death seems never satisfy'd.
Each soft sensation lost in thoughtless rage,
And breast to breast, oppos'd in furious war,
The fiery Chiefs receive the vengeful steel.
O'er lifeless heaps of men the soldiers climb
Still eager for the combat, while the ground
Made slipp'ry by the gushing streams of gore
Is treach'rous to their feet. — Oh ! horrid sight ! —
Too much for me to stand, my life was chill'd,
As from the turret I beheld the sight,
It forc'd me to retire.

EVANTHE.

What of *Arsaces?*

CLEONE.

I saw him active in the battle, now,
Like light'ning, piercing thro' the thickest foe,
Then scorning to disgrace his sword in low
Plebeian blood — loud for *Vardanes* call'd —
To meet him singly, and decide the war.

EVANTHE.

Save him, ye Gods ! oh ! all my soul is fear —
Fly, fly *Cleone*, to the tow'r again,

See how fate turns the ballance; and pursue
Arsaces with thine eye; mark ev'ry blow,
Observe if some bold villain dares to urge
His sword presumptuous at my Hero's breast.
Haste, my *Cleone*, haste, to ease my fears.

SCENE VI.

EVANTHE, alone.

Ah! — what a cruel torment is suspense!
My anxious soul is torn 'twixt love and fear,
Scarce can I please me with one fancied bliss
Which kind imagination forms, but reason,
Proud, surly reason, snatches the vain joy,
And gives me up again to sad distress.
Yet I can die, and should *Arsaces* fall
This fatal draught shall ease me of my sorrows.

SCENE VII.

CLEONE, alone.

Oh! horror! horror! horror! — cruel Gods! —
I saw him fall — I did — pierc'd thro' with wounds —
Curs'd! curs'd *Vardanes!* — hear'd the gen'ral cry,
Which burst, as tho' all nature had dissolv'd,
Hark! how they shout! the noise seems coming this way.

SCENE VIII.

ARSACES, GOTARZES, BARZAPHERNES, and OFFICERS, with VARDANES and LYSIAS, prisoners.

ARSACES.

Thanks to the ruling pow'rs who blest our arms,
Prepare the sacrifices to the Gods,
And grateful songs of tributary praise. —
Gotarzes, fly, my Brother, find *Evanthe*,
And bring the lovely mourner to my arms.

GOTARZES.

Yes, I'll obey you, with a willing speed.
(Exit GOTARZES)

ARSACES.

Thou, *Lysias*, from yon tow'r's aspiring height
Be hurl'd to death, thy impious hands are stain'd
With royal blood. — Let the traitor's body
Be giv'n to hungry dogs.

LYSIAS.

Welcome grim death ! —
I've fed thy maw with Kings, and lack no more
Revenge — Now, do thy duty Officer.

OFFICER.

Yea, and would lead all traitors gladly thus, —
The boon of their deserts.

SCENE IX.

ARSACES, VARDANES, BARZAPHERNES.

ARSACES.

But for *Vardanes*,
The Brother's name forgot —

VARDANES.

You need no more,
I know the rest — Ah ! death is near, my wounds
Permit me not to live — my breath grows short,
Curs'd be *Phraates* arm which stop'd my sword,
Ere it had reach'd thy proud exulting heart.
But the wretch paid dear for his presuming;
A just reward. —

ARSACES.

He sinks, yet bear him up —

VARDANES.

Curs'd be the multitude which o'erpow'r'd me,
And beat me to the ground, cover'd with wounds —
But, oh ! 'tis done ! my ebbing life is done —
I feel death's hand upon me — Yet, I die
Just as I wish, and daring for a crown,
Life without rule is my disdain; I scorn
To swell a haughty Brother's sneaking train,
To wait upon his ear with flatt'ring tales,
And court his smiles; come, death, in thy cold arms,
Let me forget Ambition's mighty toil,
And shun the triumphs of a hated Brother —
O ! bear me off — Let not his eyes enjoy
My agonies — My sight grows dim with death.

(They bear him off)

SCENE the Last.

ARSACES, GOTARZES, BARZAPHERNES, and EVANTHE supported.

EVANTHE.

Lead me, oh ! lead me, to my lov'd *Arsaces*,
Where is he ? —

ARSACES.

Ha ! what's this ? — Just heav'ns ! — my fears —

EVANTHE.

Arsaces, oh ! thus circl'd in thy arms,
I die without a pang.

ARSACES.

Ha ! die ? — why stare ye,
Ye lifeless ghosts ? Have none of ye a tongue
To tell me I'm undone ?

GOTARZES.

Soon, my Brother,
Too soon, you'll know it by the sad effects ;
And if my grief will yet permit my tongue
To do its office, thou shalt hear the tale.
Cleone, from the turret, view'd the battle,
And on *Phraates* fix'd her erring sight,
Thy brave unhappy friend she took for thee,
By his garb deceiv'd, which like to thine he wore.
Still with her eye she follow'd him, where-e'er
He pierc'd the foe, and to *Vardanes* sword
She saw him fall a hapless victim, then,

In agonies of grief, flew to *Evanthe*,
And told the dreadful tale — the fatal bowl
I saw —

ARSACES.

Be dumb, nor ever give again
Fear to the heart, with thy ill-boding voice.

EVANTHE.

Here, I'll rest, till death, on thy lov'd bosom,
Here let me sigh my — Oh ! the poison works —

ARSACES.

Oh ! horror ! —

EVANTHE.

Cease — this sorrow pains me more
Than all the wringing agonies of death,
The dreadful parting of the soul from, this,
Its wedded clay — Ah ! there — that pang shot thro'
My throbbing heart —

ARSACES.

Save her, ye Gods ! — oh ! save her !
And I will bribe ye with clouds of incense;
Such num'rous sacrifices, that your altars
Shall even sink beneath the mighty load.

EVANTHE.

When I am dead, dissolv'd to native dust,
Yet let me live in thy dear mem'ry —
One tear will not be much to give *Evanthe*.

ARSACES.

My eyes shall e'er two running fountains be,
And wet thy urn with everflowing tears,

Joy ne'er again within my breast shall find
A residence — Oh ! speak, once more —

EVANTHE.

Life's just out —
My Father — Oh ! protect his honour'd age,
And give him shelter from the storms of fate,
He's long been fortune's sport — Support me — Ah !—
I can no more — my glass is spent — farewel —
Forever — *Arsaces!* — Oh ! (Dies)

ARSACES.

Stay, oh ! stay,
Or take me with thee — dead ! she's cold and dead !
Her eyes are clos'd, and all my joys are flown —
Now burst ye elements, from your restraint,
Let order cease, and chaos be again.
Break ! break tough heart ! — oh ! torture — life dissolve —
Why stand ye idle ? Have I not one friend
To kindly free me from this pain ? One blow,
One friendly blow would give me ease.

BARZAPHERNES.

The Gods
Forefend ! — Pardon me, Royal Sir, if I
Dare, seemingly disloyal, seize your sword,
Despair may urge you far —

ARSACES.

Ha ! traitors ! rebels ! —
Hoary rev'rend Villain ! what, disarm me ?
Give me my sword — what, stand ye by, and see
Your Prince insulted ? Are ye rebels all ? —

BARZAPHERNES.

Be calm, my gracious Lord!

GOTARZES.

Oh! my lov'd Brother!

ARSACES.

Gotarzes too! all! all! conspir'd against me?
Still, are ye resolv'd that I must live,
And feel the momentary pangs of death? —
Ha! — this, shall make a passage for my soul —
(Snatches BARZAPHERNES' sword)
Out, out vile cares, from your distress'd abode —
(Stabs himself)

BARZAPHERNES.

Oh! ye eternal Gods!

GOTARZES.

Distraction! heav'ns!
I shall run mad —

ARSACES.

Ah! 'tis in vain to grieve —
The steel has done its part, and I'm at rest —
Gotarzes wear my crown, and be thou blest,
Cherish, *Barzaphernes*, my trusty chief —
I faint, oh! lay me by *Evanthe's* side —
Still wedded in our death's — *Bethas* —

BARZAPHERNES.

Despair,
My Lord, has broke his heart, I saw him stretch'd,
Along the flinty pavement, in his gaol —
Cold, lifeless —

ARSACES.

He's happy then — had he heard
This tale, he'd — Ah ! *Evanthe* chides my soul,
For ling'ring here so long — another pang
And all the world, adieu — oh ! adieu ! — (Dies)

GOTARZES.

Oh ! —
Fix me, heav'n, immoveable, a statue,
And free me from o'erwhelming tides of grief.

BARZAPHERNES.

Oh ! my lov'd Prince, I soon shall follow thee,
Thy laurel'd glories whither are they fled ? —
Would I had died before this fatal day ! —
Triumphant garlands pride my soul no more,
No more the lofty voice of war can charm —
And why then am I here ? Thus then —
(Offers to stab himself)

GOTARZES.

Ah ! hold,
Nor rashly urge the blow — think of me, and
Live — My heart is wrung with streaming anguish,
Tore with the smarting pangs of woe, yet, will I
Dare to live, and stem misfortune's billows.
Live then, and be the guardian of my youth,
And lead me on thro' virtue's rugged path.

BARZAPHERNES.

O, glorious youth, thy words have rous'd the
Drooping genius of my soul ; thus, let me
Clasp thee, in my aged arms ; yes, I will live —

Live, to support thee in thy kingly rights,
And when thou'rt firmly fix'd, my task's perform'd,
My honourable task — Then I'll retire,
Petition gracious heav'n to bless my work,
And in the silent grave forget my cares.

GOTARZES.

Now, to the Temple, let us onward move,
And strive t' appease the angry pow'rs above.
Fate yet may have some ills reserv'd in store,
Continu'd curses, to torment us more.
Tho', in their district, Monarchs rule alone,
Jove sways the mighty Monarch on his throne:
Nor can the shining honours which they wear,
Purchase one joy, or save them from one care.

FINIS.

www.ingramcontent.com/pod-product-compliance
Lightning Source LLC
LaVergne TN
LVHW050527100826
845148LV00002B/467

* 9 7 8 1 4 2 5 5 1 9 8 8 9 *